Every Teacher Matters

Inspiring Well-Being through Mindfulness

A portion of the proceeds from every
book sold will be donated to the
Teacher Support Network

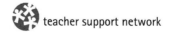 teacher support network

EVERY
TEACHER
MATTERS

Inspiring Well-Being through Mindfulness

KATHRYN LOVEWELL

Every Teacher Matters
Inspiring Well-Being through Mindfulness

First published in 2012 by

Ecademy Press
48 St Vincent Drive, St Albans, Herts, AL1 5SJ
info@ecademy-press.com
www.ecademy-press.com

Printed and bound by TJ International Ltd, Padstow, UK
Illustrations: Penny Haynes
http://www.bluebeancartoons.co.uk/
Designed by Michael Inns
Artwork by Karen Gladwell

Printed on acid-free paper from managed forests.
This book is printed on demand, so no copies will
be remaindered or pulped.

ISBN 978-1-908746-36-8

Contents

Dedication   vii

Foreword by Professor Felicia Huppert   xi

Prelude   xv

Introduction   xix

CHAPTER ONE: **Recognise your Value**   1

CHAPTER TWO: **The Diamond Within**   21

CHAPTER THREE: **Take the Oxygen First**   43

CHAPTER FOUR: **You Create the Weather**   85

CHAPTER FIVE: **The Mind-Body Connection**   99

CHAPTER SIX: **Mindful Moments Matter**   119

CHAPTER SEVEN: **It Only Takes a Moment**   139

CHAPTER EIGHT: **You Can't Stop the Waves...**   157

CHAPTER NINE: **Simple Steps**   175

About the Author   187

Testimonials   188

Dedication

*" Success is the sum of small
efforts repeated day in day out."*

Robert Collier

I dedicate this book to every teacher who shows up, no matter what! I dedicate each page to every teacher who pursued a teaching vocation, knowing that the hours were long, the pay average, and the task infinite! I dedicate each paragraph to all those teachers who lovingly put their students first without question. I dedicate each line to every teacher who chooses to work through their holidays, preparing new schemes of work, or who stays in school to rehearse or revise. I dedicate each word to the love, grace, and wisdom of the teaching champions that our society takes for granted and is quick to judge. Thank you for standing firm in your dream and pursuit to make a difference in young people's lives. It's time to bring you back into balance!

Thank you to every teacher, formal or informal, who has inspired me to scribe my beliefs and passion on paper. My mission is to ignite the education revolution so that it meets the holistic needs of *every* person in the system, as ambitious as that may be. Thank you to Liz for encouraging me to keep going, even when every door I knocked on seemed to be locked. Thank you to Liz, Mark, Mum, Super C & Dad for believing in me, especially when my self-belief was in tatters. Thank you to my beautiful boys, Oliver, Dominic and James, who have undoubtedly been my greatest teachers. Thank you Nanny and Granddad, for introducing me to Hatha yoga as a child and for planting the seeds of loving balance and holistic well-being at a tender age. Thank you to my dear friends, whose love, support and encouragement have lifted me in times of exhaustion and despair and for sharing times of love, laughter and celebration. Thank you for reflecting the inspirational qualities in me that I believe are in every brilliant teacher.

And there are still others to thank – teachers in life and the world - for the birthing of this book: Brandon Bays for opening the door to awareness, Dr John Demartini for liberating my victim mentality and showing me divine balance in all things; Gangaji for explaining to me clearly what is meant to be; Byron Katie for helping me ask meaningful questions and stop arguing with reality; Neale Donald Walsch for inspiring a fresh conversation with God; William Whitecloud and Darren Eden for re-awakening my intuition, reminding me of what's obvious and to go for what I love.

Thank you to Jon Kabat-Zinn, who so eloquently teaches how to surf. Thank you to Thich Naht Hahn whose smile brings peace, hope and inspiration. Thank you to Shamash Alidina who made Mindfulness accessible to a dummy like me. Thank you to Felicia Huppert whose humble genius demonstrates the Science of Well-being. Thank you to Professor Mark Williams who is the living embodiment of Mindfulness and inspires profound humility. Thank you to Chris Cullen and Richard Burnett who proved it was possible, meaningful and fruitful to bring Mindfulness into the school curriculum. Thank you to Dr Shanida Nataraja who brought a blissful explanation to neuroscience and the power of meditation. Thank you to Will Ryan, *Leading with a Moral Purpose*, who confirmed living from the inside out could be done in schools starting with the Head! Thank you to Masuro Emoto who's Hidden Messages in Water crystallised my beliefs.

Thank you to Topher Morrison who dared me to dream and make every day an epic adventure; to Daniel Priestley who created a process to make my dream a reality and for introducing me to Mindy Gibbins-Klein, the Book Midwife, who lovingly guided me through the beautiful birthing of this book, Mike for his patience throughout the design process and Penny for her magical illustrations that have brought ETM to life!

Thank you to my peer proofers who willingly volunteered their time and shared their expertise to make this book the best it could be, especially Mark.

Thank you to Ian for weaving his magic and helping me complete my *bridge* so masterfully.

And finally a huge, boundless thank you to the Insideout Life team - Liz, Lollie, Sally, Jan, Christopher, Tarryn and Nina - whose loving support, tireless efforts, ceaseless encouragement, and sheer hard graft have made it possible to bring teachers and students back to balance.

Foreword

A gradual and much needed change is taking place in the values and aspirations of many governments. No longer is GDP or economic growth their sole aim and the only indicator of progress. There is a growing acceptance that improving the well-being of citizens is at least as important as GDP, and arguably more so. It is increasingly widely recognised that economic growth is not an end in itself, but a means to an end – and that end is well-being.

Some commentators equate well-being with happiness, but it is more than happiness. Well-being is about living life well – about developing our full potential as individuals and in relationship with others, and contributing to our society. Well-being, in short, is about flourishing.

Imagine an organisation, a society, or a nation, most of whose mentors were flourishing. Such a group would be characterised by creativity and innovation, by good health and vitality, by harmonious relationships, and by care for all living beings and the needs of future generations. This is the vision and aspiration proposed by the recent UN High Level Meeting on Happiness and Well-being, which took place on 2 April 2012. The UN is advocating a new economic paradigm with well-being at its core.

How can we make progress towards this vision? The most effective way, surely, is to equip our children with the skills to live life well – with the skills to flourish. Academic knowledge and traditional educational content have an important role to play, but a whole child approach is crucial if we want our children to flourish. We must consider not just their cognitive development, but their emotional, social, moral and spiritual development. And because each child is unique, we must consider their individual interests and passions, their strengths and talents – their inner spark.

This is not new. The rhetoric that "every child matters" has had currency for some time in the educational context. What is new is its growing prominence in the broader social context, and the growing determination to move from rhetoric to making it a reality.

This is where Kathryn Lovewell's book has such a powerful role to play. If every child matters, then it must follow as night follows day that every teacher matters. In most developed countries, children will have spent in excess of 10,000 hours at school, and this provides an unparalleled opportunity to nurture the whole child, and to develop their full potential to live life well. But harnessing this opportunity requires that we take care of our teachers. For children to flourish, we need teachers who are flourishing.

This book describes the many barriers to teacher flourishing in our current educational systems, but its core message is a simple, evidence-based approach that promotes flourishing. The practice of mindfulness in the teacher's own life, and its extension to mindful teaching, can be transformative. Mindfulness is a particular way of paying attention to what is going on in the moment in the mind, in the body and in our immediate surroundings. We learn to pay attention to our experiences with curiosity and with kindness – kindness towards ourselves and others. These qualities help to create clarity about what we are experiencing, and to respond appropriately rather than reacting automatically.

Some teachers seem naturally to embody mindfulness, and it almost certainly makes them fine teachers. But mindfulness is a set of skills that can be learnt by all. These skills are described in a highly approachable and delightful way in Lovewell's book. There can be no doubt that practising these skills and becoming a mindful individual and a mindful teacher, has the power to transform the teaching experience and the lives of the children we entrust to our teachers for all those thousands of hours. The promotion of flourishing through mindful education may contribute in no small way to realising the UN vision of a world characterised by sustainable well-being.

Felicia A Huppert
Professor of Psychology
Director of the Well-being Institute
University of Cambridge

Prelude

" Sometimes it is more important
to be kind than right."

Brandon Bays

I began formal teaching (in state secondary schools) because I loved my subjects, Drama and Art, and I loved inspiring young people. I left mainstream education because I felt so frustrated with a system that seemed to have forgotten that its A-to-C statistics were human beings and so were the teachers! The qualifications sausage machine was squeezing out more and more exams with less and less regard for the well-being of its learners. Its inflexibility and lack of space and time in the curriculum to create a holistic provision drove me to do something about it. I wanted to make a difference as a teacher – a positive difference to the young people I taught. Each day I felt more and more thwarted as the legislation just got tighter and tighter. Suicide rates for young people, especially young men, are alarmingly high; dropout rates are disturbing; obesity in young people is at crisis levels; and mental health for children is a pressing concern throughout the nation. Many are the symptoms of crisis: young people out of balance, out of touch with themselves and their magnificence, despondent, and unaware of the significant contributions they can make. Teachers are at the front line of this pain, and they are the ones who need the emotional and social competence to cope with and manage this plight among children and young people.

According to the United Nations children's organization, UNICEF, in its 2007 study – Child Poverty in Perspective: An Overview of Child Well-being in Rich Countries - *exposed how the U.K. is failing its children, coming* **bottom of the league table for child well-being among 21 industrialised countries.**

Moreover, the U.K. ranks in the bottom third in five of the six categories covered: material well-being, family and peer relationships, health and safety, behaviour and risks, educational well-being, and children's subjective sense of well-being.

As Children's Commissioner for England, Professor Sir Al Aynsley-Green, noted: "We are turning out a generation of young people who are unhappy, unhealthy, engaging in risky behaviour, who have poor relationships with their family and their peers, who have low expectations and don't feel safe."

It doesn't take a genius to recognise something needs to change – I'm not talking about a little tweak in the curriculum here and there. I mean a genuine shift in mindset as to the health and well-being of young people and of the entire education system.

As *Insideout Life* developed our programmes in schools, it dramatically shifted focus from student to teacher. Every time we came in to support the students, the teachers would look pleadingly at us and ask "what about us?" It became painfully obvious that unless we take care of the teachers, the state of our children would continue to decline. What is required is a 'whole school' shift; otherwise we are only scraping the surface of making real and lasting change.

Every Teacher Matters is the starting point for this seismic shift. When we support the people that have one of the most significant impacts on youngsters and teach them emotional resilience tools - not only to cope with their day, but to pass on to their wards – then we have a powerful fresh focus for holistic well-being in schools.

I believe Mindful Awareness Practices (MAP) are the key to unlocking sustained health and happiness in schools. *Every Teacher Matters* is one of the steps in implementing this shift. May it inspire a new respect and appreciation for the significance and power of educators and the role of education in our world.

Introduction

"Education is the great engine of personal development. It is through education that the daughter of a peasant can become a doctor, that the son of a mineworker can become head of the mine, and that a child of farm workers can become president of a great nation."

Nelson Mandela

The purpose of this book is to demonstrate why every teacher matters. It serves to honour every teacher in the world and to recognise the immense value each contributes to inspiring our future leaders. It is a gentle introduction to a new paradigm in personal and classroom management. It introduces Mindfulness as a means to bring balance to the hearts and minds of both teacher and student.

I coin the phrase *Mindful Teacher*. A Mindful teacher is one who not only practises the art of Mindfulness for herself, but also threads Mindful Awareness Practices throughout her lesson. This will empower her not only to manage stress but also to enrich learning. This book offers an alternative to fear-based school discipline and promotes a peaceful approach to teaching-and-learning relationships. It is not a quick fix to the system of highly pressured, demanding, and relentless measurement of education. It is rather a springboard into a fresh approach that acknowledges and supports those at the forefront of cultivating minds.

Teachers are the "parents/carers/mentors" outside the home. They generally spend more time with the children than the parents do. Society recognises how significant parental guidance is for children and young people and yet ignores the school carer/mentors, ignores their emotional health and well-being, and often disregards the importance of their physical health too. Schooling carer/mentors have a profound impact on our children, positive and negative. It is time to ensure that every teacher is trained not only to cope with the insane pressures of teaching, but also to understand and manage the emotional demands.

> *"Society's expectation that teachers manage the emotional lives of their students as well as teach subject matter may leave many teachers exhausted and burnt out."*
>
> (Hargreaves 1998)

Teachers need to take care of themselves or they are simply not fit for purpose, and it is imperative they are taught the practical skills both to cope with the raw emotion that often arises in the classroom and to wholesomely support a child or young person in crisis or who is simply struggling with being in his or her own skin. Surely education must, first and foremost, ensure its learners are well-rounded, wholesome, healthy (in mind and body) human *beings*. From these, successful achievement naturally follows.

Every Teacher Matters is a springboard for training in emotional health and well-being for teachers. There are a myriad of ways to inspire well-being. Felicia Huppert PhD, Professor of Psychology and Director of the Cambridge Well-being Institute, has been exploring these in depth for many years. Her research findings provide powerful evidence supporting the positive influence of Mindfulness in our twenty-first century frenetic world. In the *Science of well-being* she, along with Dr. Nick Bayliss and Professor Barry Keverne, provide a stimulating overview for enhancing well-being, both for ourselves and for our communities. Mindfulness is, I believe, a tool that brings about wholeness and balance like no other.

To genuinely support a teacher, we need to understand exactly what a teacher does. So let's examine this role. To state the obvious, a teacher teaches! To teach, as defined by the Encarta Dictionary, means:

1 **to impart knowledge or skill to somebody by instruction or example**

Your job is to be in the best state to impart your knowledge; to be clear, alert and inspirational in your delivery. Your job is to *be* the best example you can be; to walk your talk, to love learning, to love being in your classroom, and ultimately to love imparting your experience and knowledge with enthusiasm and energy.

2 **to give lessons in or provide information about a subject**

Your job is give exciting and stimulating lessons where your subject comes alive for your students and, no matter what that subject is, to exude life teachings. Your manner, your demeanour, your attitude and your approach to life, learning, stressful situations, demands, questions and challenging behaviour sends a message louder and clearer than any prescribed curriculum. You need to be fit for purpose!

3 **to give lessons to a person (or animal)**

Your job is to educate a *person*, a human being, a child. You have the privileged position to open and touch the mind and heart of a young person. You are connecting with a magical entity. You are not programming a computer. You are working with a whole person. Their mind, heart and body are influenced and filter everything they observe about you. What you do in every moment impacts all aspects of who they are. You are faced with all facets of the person, not just their best parts, not just their clever parts, not just their well-behaved parts. You need to be equipped to manage and sustain the depth of provision that is required to meet the holistic needs of every young person you come into contact with.

4 to bring understanding of something to somebody, especially through an experience

What better gift can one person offer another, than to bring understanding? The ultimate understanding is that of the self and where that person fits into the puzzle of life. Your experience of life has a unique flavour, and this unique awareness provides a unique opportunity to share your discoveries through experiential sharing. With understanding comes healthy choices and balanced perspective.

5 to be a teacher in an institution

You belong to a vast organisation. You belong to a community far bigger than your school community. You are part of a global family. You have the opportunity to share and learn from each other rather than compare and compete! An institution is defined as a large organisation that is influential in the community. You play a significant part in your community. You are part of the ultimate service industry! The way you "give service" is hugely significant and impacts every person you teach and work with. This power can be wielded with rigidity and force or with grace, compassion and inspiration. It's your choice. What if the institution of education was liberated from its micro-agendas and came together to focus on one teaching message – that of love!

6 to advocate or preach something

An advocate is someone who supports or speaks in favour of something. What are you in favour of? What do you want to be remembered for – acts of kindness, being inspirational, making a difference......? An advocate is someone who acts or intercedes on behalf of another. What if your best teaching moment was outside the classroom, maybe in the playground, in the corridor, on the sports field, or in the head teacher's office? You play a vital role in building resilience in every child. You nurture self-worth, self-belief and courage. You are the one on the front line meeting head-on the trials and tribulations that children face in the twenty-first century. It is your intercession that may keep a child in school when all they want to do is run away. It is your guidance that may make the difference between self-harm and seeking help. It is your assistance that may influence a child's life choices between truth and deceit. It is your support that they turn to when they don't know where else to turn. You need to be fit. You need to be well, and you need to feel strong. You need to be strong enough to stand with them in their sorrow, in their confusion and in their pain; courageous enough to hold their hand and their heart when life knocks them so off balance that they see nothing but despair; compassionate enough to permit their rage and frustration; and kind enough to facilitate gentle guidance with kindness and humility.

Every Child Matters (ECM), a U.K. government initiative for England and Wales that was launched in 2003, rightly brought attention to the needs of the child. These needs continue to change at an accelerating pace, and twenty-first century life brings with it a whole new landscape of challenges. But just as importantly, I believe, **Every Teacher Matters!** Without the needs of the teacher being met, who will be there to attend to the needs of the children? Unless a holistic and supportive approach is taken in schools to take care of the teachers and children alike, the institution will eventually disintegrate. Teachers are one of *the* most influential mentors of a child's life and deserve support, guidance, encouragement and praise (as does the child).

So what if we applied the five ECM Outcomes to teachers?

Every teacher deserves to be healthy.

You deserve to feel healthy in mind, body and soul. You need a break at break time; you need fresh air, exercise and nutritious food at lunch time. You need to drink water regularly and ensure your brain and body are hydrated. You need to have a rest at the weekend and time to relax in the evening. You need to have time and energy to socialise with family and friends to ensure mental and emotional health is maintained and stress alleviated.

Every teacher deserves to stay safe.

To feel emotionally as well as physically safe is imperative. No teacher should have to face a barrage of abuse, feel intimidated, or be threatened. You deserve to feel confident in your space and know that you will be supported and protected whilst in school. Every teacher deserves to feel they have someone to confide in, someone to guide them, someone to help them when life serves them a tsunami. You deserve a supportive Senior Leadership Team; one that has time for you and reassures you your position is safe.

Every teacher deserves to enjoy and achieve.

Feeling satisfaction for a great day's work, inspiring minds and opening hearts to the wonders of the world, is a right of every person who has worked hard to earn the title of teacher. You deserve to be enriched with regular support and training to ensure you remain inspired and balanced. Your personal development is beneficial to a child's personal development. As you discover new techniques, new approaches and new methods for teaching and delivering your subject matter, every child will be rewarded with fresh ideas and new perspectives. The techniques I have been delivering in schools and prison education for over three years now serve to enhance and enrich everything you already know. You deserve this enrichment. You deserve to progress as a learner and a thought leader in your classroom! You deserve to enjoy every moment of your teaching day!

Every teacher deserves to make a positive contribution.

What is life if not to contribute? Every teacher makes a difference. It is your choice whether it is positive. Every teacher, through the rigour of your training, has earned the right to inspire your learners with their natural creativity, inspiration and gifts. Every teacher deserves to have the freedom to tune in to their natural wisdom and teach the way that inspires them and their students (without being pinned down by government initiatives that regularly shift.) Every teacher deserves to connect with their intuition and to scrap their lesson plan if their students are not in the right state to learn (for a myriad of reasons) and to meet the needs of their students as they deem fit in that moment.

Every teacher deserves to achieve economic well-being.

Every teacher deserves a salary that reflects the knowledge, skill, experience and substantial influence they have in society. The impact a teacher has on the potential leaders (and offenders) of this world is vast. Every teacher deserves recognition. The pay scale ought to reflect the demanding nature of the profession and the "on-call" nature of the job. When is a teacher's job done? Never! There is always something more that can be done, prepared, researched.... At the time of writing, our economy is still highly volatile. It is vital to provide a stable and secure platform for teachers to inspire the leaders of tomorrow. If teachers are preoccupied with personal worries about paying bills, where to live, and if they can afford to move to the area where they want to teach, they are less likely to be fully present in the classroom. Every teacher deserves a wage that represents their ongoing and longstanding value to society. I believe teachers are priceless, but for now, let's settle for a fair income!

> *"Modern cynics and sceptics see no harm in paying those to whom they entrust the minds of their children a smaller wage than is paid to those to whom they entrust the care of their plumbing."*
> John F. Kennedy

You may already know everything in this book. I believe you already intuitively "know" and do magical things in your classroom, but for those who are struggling with the pace, the relentless pressure of targets and judging success on measurements that may not be suitable for every child; I invite you to stay with me. This book is an easy read.

It simply offers a gentle reminder to take the oxygen first and provides Mindful first steps by which to do this. My *Getting in The Right State* training programmes provide a practical implementation of the techniques, but first I feel it is important to reflect and acknowledge why these powerful tools might be worth learning.

For the purposes of this book, I refer to the teacher in the feminine, not (just) because I am female, but because the majority of (primary) school teachers are women and I would love to honour them. It is also believed that women teachers are *"more affected by teacher stress than men"* (Santiago et al., 2008) But, in the interests of balance, I shall refer to the learner, student, or child in the masculine.

I am writing this for you, the teacher. If you are not a teacher in the formal sense, please embrace the title for this moment. You are a teacher to someone, just not necessarily in the classroom.

Throughout this book, you will encounter the Wave.

This Wave is your invitation to dive into the world of creativity and imagination. It is your opportunity to taste Mindfulness meditation and/or creative visualisation; to take a moment to stop, breathe, be still and fully present.

I sincerely hope you enjoy my stories that aim to inspire and prepare newly qualified teachers (NQT) and to reignite the passion of established, experienced teachers. This book is dedicated to your tireless and loving dedication to your craft and the children you teach.

CHAPTER ONE

Recognise your Value

Recognise your Value

" A teacher affects eternity:
he can never tell when his influence stops. "

Henry Adams

You Make a Difference in Every Moment!

If I asked you to quantify the value you offer in the classroom, what would you say? If society were to place a price tag on the value you provide in the community, what would it be? Isn't it interesting that our materialistic world is so quick to pass judgement on a product or service by assessing how much you the consumer are willing to pay for it? How much are you willing to pay for the latest I-gadget? How much is a new hair style really worth to you? What about your health and well-being?

You, the teacher, the provider of inspiration and knowledge, are priceless. Aside from the impact parents have, there is no-one more valuable to our society and culture than our teachers. You, the teacher, are a remarkable and valuable commodity.

You are all things to your young learners: mother, nurse, social worker, mediator, nose-wiper (hopefully just for the littlies!), peace-keeper, friend, and unfortunately sometimes, police officer! Until you become a teacher you can have absolutely no idea what this incredible vocation entails; the multiple hats you wear during the course of one day, the multiple roles you play in the school, and the multiple personalities you develop as you juggle your passion for teaching and your life outside the school gates. Let's face it: you are amazing!

As a teacher with decades of experience inside and outside mainstream education and within Her Majesty's prison system, I believe **praise** is one of the most significant keys to happy learners, successful understanding, and progress. So let's start with that! When encouraging my students to critique a performance (drama being my first love!), I would always ask them to give an "appraisal" of what they saw. They knew that the word appraisal had a special word within it for which I was listening. If they started off with a criticism – so easy to give –then I would stop them and ask them to ap*praise* again. They knew I would only hear the positive first. Let's be honest. If you've just put your ego, personality and street cred on the line, would you want to be shot down in the first breath?

Interesting correlation: performer – teacher. That's exactly what you do, every day. You stand up in front of a potentially mixed audience (some friend, some foe) and you take risks to engage your audience and keep them not only entertained, but also inspired to take action! You use your body language, your voice, your facial expressions to connect with your audience and bring them to a place of understanding, empathy even, and then Bam! You have them eating out of the palm of your hand, soaking up learning gems like sponges. At times during your performance you may have to reel in some of the audience who are losing interest; you may need to start telling jokes, juggle some knives, dazzle them with a magic trick or maybe even crack the whip! Whatever your strategy, you do it, day after day, term after term, year after year, because you know (even when the road is rough and tough) you make a difference in every moment to these young hearts. So let's big it up for teachers. **You rock!**

If you are a non-teacher reading this book, you may be wondering what all the fuss is about. I know, I know, teachers have it easy. They only work half a day and they have so many holidays and oh my, the summer holiday – well that's just obscene! Well, a teacher may be officially "on duty" from say 8.00 till 3.30ish, say an average of seven and a half hours. That's when the performer is performing all her tricks. The juggling however doesn't end when the curtain falls at the end of the day. How do you think this great performer learns her lines, choreographs the dances, designs the scenery, prepares her stage for the next performance? If she's lucky she has a Teaching Assistant who helps make props and rearranges the stage; and if she is fortunate enough to have a great creative director, head of department, or head teacher, that will also make a huge difference to her rehearsal process. But ultimately it's down to her to put on the show and make it razzle-dazzle so that her customers buy a ticket for the next performance and show up even if it's raining.

Have you ever tried to put on a show? It takes balls! It takes commitment, courage, faith, self-belief, and more sweat and tears than you can possibly imagine. Hands up you newbie teachers (NQTs) who are willing to admit they've shed a tear or 10 just preparing their lessons plans, never mind when the entire lesson has fallen flat on its face! And, so that you feel included, how about you amazing old-timers who have chosen to move on and seek a fresh challenge, only to discover your amazing classroom management doesn't work in this part of town?

Back to the performance. Have you ever stood up in front of anyone in the hopes of impressing them or connecting with them? You know just how terrifying a job interview can be, and that's usually with just a few people – try thirty! Now add into the mix that you are their eighth teacher that term and they really aren't interested in listening to you or building a relationship with you on any level "coz you're bound to bugger off" sooner rather than later.

So what is it that you offer as a teacher?

Let's explore what a Mindful teacher provides for the child if successful learning is going to take place. Firstly, you offer **safety**. You provide a safe and nurturing environment in which to learn. The child needs to feel safe. If the child feels safe, he or she will be able to explore his learning capacity to the max. He will be willing to take risks and know it is safe to make mistakes. He will feel safe to push the boundaries to a healthy degree and understand when to stop and why. This safety is a key to a child wanting to enter your classroom and stay there. Clear boundaries are put in place, giving them clarity and comfort, so they know what is expected of them and how to behave. A Mindful teacher can set clear boundaries in a supportive and loving manner, guiding them literally to stop, look, listen and think, just like the green cross code. It's beautifully clear and simple. They know it will keep them safe and ultimately alive!

What else do you offer? The next obvious gift is **knowledge**; you teach them. The key to effective teaching is of course that the learner learns! How do you do this? Simple! You **inspire** them! If you are a teacher you'll know inspiration can come in all shapes and sizes. The beauty of you is that you are unique. Because of your unique qualities, it is impossible to quantify how you capture the imaginations of thirty-plus children, who often have different beliefs, family structures, upbringings and aspirations, but by some miracle you do! Realistically, you may not catch all the fish in one net first go, but over time you have the skill to decipher their highest values and hook them in. A Mindful teacher will instinctively know how to hunt for clues and work out what makes each child tick, so that you can hook them in with what brings them alive. Now, due to the demands of the curriculum, this may not always be possible, but for the purposes of understanding the multi-skills required to be an effective teacher, we shall focus on the human, rather than the system, for now.

A Mindful teacher will **support** their student. I know it goes without saying, but when we explore Mindfulness in depth, you will understand the importance of non-judgement. This is a real challenge for a teacher who is highly pressured and has demands coming at her from all sides. Taking time to support a child when they are struggling, either academically or emotionally, is the biggest privilege a teacher can have and often the biggest challenge.

I'll make the assumption that you have the skills to translate the confusing and nonsensical subject be it conjunctives, algebra, or poetry into "Barry" language, so that Barry can not only comprehend it but also apply the new knowledge meaningfully. Supporting a child emotionally is a whole other ball game. You may or may not have experienced what the child is going through, and ultimately no-one can really understand what another person is experiencing because of their unique emotional filters and personal history. The beauty of a Mindful teacher is that she is at least aware of this and can express support with compassion and without judgement or trying to "fix".

This may seem a big leap, but trust me on this and suspend your disbelief till the end of the book. The child is already perfect; so are you; so is the situation. The challenge is to reveal this to the child so that he becomes self empowered to discover the solution for himself. (I'm sure you can think of many examples where this statement is an oversimplification. There will, of course, be situations such as abuse and protection that will require additional skills and sensitivity. However, I stand by the premise that each child (and teacher) is pristine, perfect inside, no matter what's showing up behaviourally on the outside.)

The Mindful teacher may offer possible solutions and guidance, but ultimately returning the power to the child is the key to their awakening or, like the Green Cross Code, their survival. We will explore EQ, Emotional Intelligence, in depth and connect the need to develop EQ in both you, the teacher, and the learner, so that school becomes the foundation for Mindful, joyful learning and living. The purpose of this book is to build awareness of the intense value of Emotional Health inside and outside the classroom. If we are teaching and learning from an emotionally healthy place, then great outcomes will arise in terms of relationships, learning, achievement and well-being!

A Mindful teacher will **guide** a student. The Montessori Way is a great example of trusting a child's learning ability. A study comparing state school to Montessori schooling demonstrated significantly superior social, emotional and cognitive development... thus revealing an effective model to help students self-regulate. (Lillard & Else-Quest, 2005) I'm not advocating a particular style of teaching; there are pros and cons to every modality. However, the premise that we guide our students rather than dictate to them, when it relates to their internal health and creative wealth, is imperative.

As the years fly by, there is so much pressure to perform and improve league tables that the child is given little leeway to explore, investigate, make mistakes, or discover for himself. The 1800s Victorian learning style by rote is often inevitable to ensure targets are hit and deadlines are met. This leaves the child disempowered, disillusioned, and often completely disinterested. Oh, and did I mention it's boring, and not just for the child, I might add!? So a Mindful teacher has the gift of guiding her students to discover new and exciting things. Not all subjects will light the fires of every child, but anything taught with enthusiasm and Heartfulness will touch the imagination of the child.

There are of course many other qualities that you as a teacher have that will make the learning experience significant, meaningful, and fun for the child. I don't need to harp on about all these; you know what they are and how you do it. For now, I invite you to stop just for a moment, simply close your eyes, and pause. Bring all your attention to your heart and connect with your unique qualities; your unique ways to engage your delicious rabble. Recall all the ways you go the extra mile: phoning parents; helping children after school; spending countless hours in rehearsal long after the school day has ended, putting on a production that they will remember for the rest of their lives because you made it special; running your little heart out on the sports field in the teachers' three-legged race; looking funky grooving on down at the school disco; enduring cold, wet sponges being flung at you at the summer fete; and even being willing to be gunked with green slime in front of the entire school and parents...... Just take three deep breaths and let down the protective armour that stops you from praising yourself.

There is no need to feel bashful. You are a tall poppy, and you are here to celebrate in this moment the magnificence of who you are and what you offer every day in that amazing haven of learning we call the classroom. Invite your heart to open and be willing to receive and acknowledge the genuine praise that you deserve. If it feels uncomfortable, let that be okay, and let the feelings of awkwardness and "arw it's nothing" wash through you and let them go.

 Breathe in the feelings *of gratitude from all the children you have taught or will teach in the future and from their parents.*

 Breathe in the power *of the unique student-teacher connection and acknowledge your skill and sensitivity as a human being dressed up in teacher's clothing.*

 Breathe in the joy *of building respectful relationships that blossom and grow and may stay in the hearts of your learners forever.*

 Breathe in the magic *that you inspire, bringing a subject alive in your own unique way.*

 Breathe in the love *you bring to your children and your teaching.*

Just stop and notice without judgement just how beautiful you are and how priceless your job is. And smile.....

The Serenity Jar

The Serenity Jar is a simple way of representing our inner life. I use a real Jar as an effective teaching tool so that you can literally visualise the machinations of your heart and mind. It is a three-dimensional representation of what is happening inside you and how you can not only manage your stress effectively, but also reduce your stress long-term through Mindfulness. If you've never trained with me, you won't have seen my Serenity Jar. Here's a chance to explore this powerful metaphor.

Imagine a clear Jar with a lid. The Jar has water, dirt and glitter in it. The water is you. It has many similar qualities to a diamond. It is clear, pure, pristine and calm. The dirt is all your unresolved history; the negative beliefs and internal stories you tell yourself, past hurt and unforgiven memories. The glitter represents your diamond, the best part of you, your inner sparkle. The part of you that exceeds all expectations in times of crisis; the part of you that opens your heart to a stranger in need, and the part of you that can find understanding, forgiveness and balance even in conflict.

Imagine The Jar at rest and untouched on level ground. The water is clear, still and pure. This is your natural state, the state you were born as, the state you wish, hope and intend to live in. This is your desired outcome after practising Mindful methods. As a Mindful teacher, when you leave for school, your aim is to begin the day in this state. When you begin your lesson, this is how you want to commence teaching. When you go to bed at night, this is the state you want to relax into before you sleep. You are tranquil and still. You are clear, calm and fluid.

However, when something unexpected happens, when someone speaks out of turn or your buttons get pushed, it only takes a little nudge of The Jar to unsettle the dirt. If you imagine the water now, you will already have cloudy water. This is for the minor irritations in your day. Someone didn't say please or thank you, your Head of Department called a meeting without notice, a student gave you "a look".... Already, your water is unsettled and cloudy. Now imagine a bigger "threat" to your equilibrium. You're about to be observed, you've mislaid an exam paper, you've just heard Ofsted (Office for Standards in Education) are coming in!!! What's happened to your Jar now? This may be quite a shakeup for you, and the dirt is swirling throughout the water. It is getting darker and even more difficult to see through. Now take the ultimate step into a stressful situation: a student is screaming and swearing at you, a colleague has just humiliated you in front of your students or you've just been told your contract isn't being renewed. Your Jar is well and truly stirred. The dirt is everywhere. There is chaos in the Jar. It is like a tornado inside. The water is filthy. You cannot see anything but mud and mess. Your vision is clouded. You cannot see through. There is inner turmoil and chaos.

"My mind is troubled, like a fountain stirred,
And I myself see not the bottom of it."

William Shakespeare

In this state, you cannot see where you are going. You have absolutely no idea what direction you are going in. It is impossible to see clearly, think, or act with clarity. Your judgement is clouded. For years, I naively thought I could literally soldier on in this state. I thought I could keep going and everything would be ok, that I would be ok. The reality was that if I kept pushing through the mess without giving myself any time to stop, breath, be still, I would end up crashing into things, damaging myself and potentially hurting other people in the process. It was never my intention, but when we are in a state such as this, it is very hard to make sound decisions, communicate clearly, or take healthy action.

For a long time, I thought I had to get rid of the dirt to be the person I wanted to be. I thought I had to clear out all my s**t before I could live as a shining example. I thought I had to have crystal clear sparkly water to live as the diamond I knew was inside. I set to work, clearing out the garbage that no longer served me. I started digging out the old beliefs that sabotaged my thinking and my behaviours. Thanks to Brandon Bays and *The Journey*® processes, I discovered a whole new realm of love and liberation. However, over time I began to realise that there was divine balance in the "brown stuff". Dr. John Demartini's *The Breakthrough Experience* showed me that everything was in perfect balance; it was simply my perspective that needed realigning. I began to unravel how each of the experiences I had labelled s**tty were in fact a blessing. With a bigger picture approach and the willingness to see both sides (negative and positive), I began to see my dirt as treasure. The dirt was transforming into rich compost for the garden of my mind. As my new, wholesome perspective flourished, so the weeds withered, and I had space to plant flowers.

When you allow the dirt to settle, you create a space for new seeds to grow. You can plant magical seeds of understanding for an abundance of beautiful flowers to grow. You have rich colours and soothing aromas to enjoy.

The Jar simply reminds you that unless you take time to stop, to breathe, and to allow the dirt to settle (even if it's just for a moment), you are likely to land in trouble, either mentally, emotionally or literally. You may speak out of turn, say something you don't really mean, or act out of frustration or limited perspective. This neither serves you nor the recipient of the behaviour.

Give yourself permission to let the dust settle. Give yourself a chance to catch your breath. Give yourself timeout and permission to move away from the situation if possible or, if not, simply to take a deep breath (perhaps ask the person to stop shouting) and take your time to "manage" the situation. You probably already know lots of great self-management or assertiveness techniques. Great! Use them! Use whatever works for you.

The Jar is simply there to remind you that you respond more healthily from a place of Stillness. If you regularly practise bringing yourself to this state of awareness, you are more likely to be able to draw on it in times of challenge. It's like a bank account. The more deposits you put in, the more you have to draw from when you need to. You will have reserves for those unexpected emergencies. And in the frenetic, demanding world of teaching, you need all the help you can get!

If you have a Serenity Jar, use it to remind yourself to take a breath and take a moment for yourself, even if it's in the classroom. In fact, especially if it's in the classroom! You can use The Jar as a teaching tool. (Just ensure it's plastic!) If your students are bouncing off the walls for whatever reason, you can invite them to watch the Jar. You may even like to use it as a reward for a child to be the shaker of The Jar! Invite your students to pay attention to the dirt softly falling to the bottom of the Jar. Invite them to notice how smoothly it falls and to observe the water gently and slowly clearing. Depending on your Jar recipe, the dirt-to-water ratio, your water can clear quickly or slowly.

If you do not have a Jar handy, but have taught your children the technique, they can use their imagination to bring themselves to a settled state, employing the *Power Breath* (explained in Chapter 7) simultaneously. And of course, you can do this for yourself at anytime too. It's a great way to halt stressful thoughts, feelings and body reactions, and to bring yourself to the present moment. Remember the present is where peace is. If you go to the past, you get tangled in guilt and shame (should've, could've, would've, didn't), and if you leap into the future, you can drown in fear (what if this happens, what if that doesn't happen?).

The Present Moment is a place of freedom. There is nothing but peace here. Right Here, Right Now. This is all you really have. Be present to it, and rest in its embrace. Keep The Serenity Jar on your desk at school to help you re-mind yourself to breathe, be still, and let things settle. Good luck!

What You Offer as a Colleague

Recognising your value in education goes much further than simply your teaching qualifications. Like any vocation, you make a difference to the people you work with as well the people for whom you work. How you interact with your colleagues can make or break your experience in any job, but when it comes to teaching, it is imperative that you have a supportive team and that you are part of that support network for others. A Mindful teacher will ensure she takes good care of herself (I will cover this in depth in Chapter 3), and she will also take good care of her colleagues. She understands the value of a healthy team - healthy in terms of academic guidance, creative sparring, sharing of best practice and, of course, emotional support through times of personal challenge.

I was exceptionally blessed to have three awesome mentors when I went into mainstream teaching. I knew two out of three of them prior to teaching and was invited to train/teach on the job on their recommendation. Both were former teachers of mine, and I undertook my training at my old school!

My Art mentor was a fabulously talented and eccentric teacher. I understand now that perhaps she was hard on me (in my perception!)

when I was a student because she believed I could achieve something in her subject. To this day, she is a dear friend and has always been the one I go to for advice on which path to take in my career.

My Head-of-Faculty mentor was a formidable woman and not to be trifled with. She made her expectations clear, was highly disciplined and conscientious, and expected the same from me. Thanks to her, I fell in love with the authors she taught, and to this day I still highlight all the juicy and inspirational quotes in my books, just like she taught me for 'O'-Level English. (Yes she taught me as a student and then trained me as a teacher!) I loved working under her, as it ensured I kept raising my personal bar and stretched myself.

My Drama mentor and I connected on the first day we met. She was a brilliant mentor super fun, creative, and very clever. She was the master of diplomacy, of which I had much to learn, and I still think of her when I feel my blood boiling about something or someone! Although she would not label herself a Mindful teacher in the manner in which I am exploring, she was always Mindful in the purest sense. She was kind, thoughtful, non-judgemental, compassionate, and taught from the heart. I couldn't have had a better grounding in how to be an inspirational, compassionate teacher.

My early teaching career really is a celebration. I was deeply blessed to be guided by three talented and special women. I didn't fully appreciate this until I moved schools. Only then did I realise how special my time had been. By the time I taught in my last mainstream school, I was working for a tyrannical head of department and a nebulous deputy. The contrast couldn't be starker. I use these examples because they are real. You will have your own examples of inspirational and tyrannical colleagues. My invitation is that you be the best you can be, that you lead the way in supporting your colleagues, especially if they are new to education, and be the guiding light that they need in the highly pressured world of teaching. Your support could make or break a teaching career.

The Daily Telegraph reports (11th August, 2011) that more than a third of teachers who qualified in 2010 either left teaching or went into the private system within 6 months, based on study by Smithers & Robinson from Buckingham University.

So what if you were to take a moment, stop, be still, and relax. Close your eyes and imagine the perfect colleague. What does she look like? How does she walk, talk, and behave in the staff room? What does she wear, and what's her time-keeping like? Does she keep her promises? Does she go the extra mile? Is she thoughtful, supportive and helpful? See her in her full glory, not taking herself too seriously and willing to have a laugh. Know that you are her in all your greatness. Feel yourself growing taller, knowing you are the teacher others admire and aspire to. You are the one others go to for advice, and you are the one who is Mindful to take care of herself as well as her colleagues. You are a mirror and can reflect your heartfulness to others. They will all be juggling their hectic lives just as much as you. Remember to bring the sunshine into the staff room as well as your classroom. Make a difference like only you know how.

What You Offer as a Member of Your Community.

As a teacher and as a member of the community, you may take the education system for granted. Well, why wouldn't you? If you've grown up in the U.K., you've grown up with its education system. It's always been available to you and your parents and your parents' parents. It may have changed a little here and there, but ultimately it is an institution that has been part of our society since time immemorial.

Thank heavens, though, that we're not in the Victorian era; education has moved on somewhat from the caning and slipper-lashing days. Nevertheless, the "it-never-did-me-any-harm" attitude, such as my Dad supports, prevails to this day. When I'd come home and tell him of some of the toe-curling tales of poor behaviour and rudeness I experienced as a teacher, he would regularly suggest I invest in a cattle prod for a 21st-century classroom management approach. Mindful teaching hasn't fully touched his heart just yet, but I'm working on him!

So what is it you offer by being part of the education system? Each community is unique, and each school offers something unique to that community. As Will Ryan describes in his fantastic book, *Leadership with a Moral Purpose,* an Insideout School will respond to the specific needs of their community; the head teacher will tune in to the ever-changing needs of the pupils, listen to the unique requirements of the children and parents within the community, and respond accordingly.

As part of this system, you and your school create order and structure for your community. You are the bedrock of learning; foundational learning. You bring a community together and unify people from all walks of life and various cultures. You create a hub for learning and help develop lifelong skills to support children and parents to grow and learn. You provide building blocks for sharing, caring and giving. I know you know all this; I'm just reminding you.

> "When teachers foster a sense of community in their classrooms, students exhibit a more prosocial orientation (cooperative, helpful, concern for others), resulting in fewer disruptive behaviours."
>
> (Battistich, Solomon, Watson, & Schaps, 1997)

I went to my youngest son's school fair yesterday. Boys and girls alike radiated the fun and joy they were having as they danced and played. Now this is what school should be about, I thought. The joy of learning! The joy of being together! The joy of revealing talent and demonstrating team work. The joy of performing as a group. The joy of sharing, giving and receiving.

Yes, school is about developing our children's understanding of things in the world and their ability to make sense of it. But it is also about relationships, having fun, being part of a community, learning how to share, give, and help others. The fair is the epitome of the real meaning and purpose of school. It brings the diverse community together. It brings all abilities, all demographics, and all cultures together. There are no boundaries and no limitations. Everyone comes to gather to have fun, to contribute in lots of different ways, and to celebrate their school togetherness. The teachers are amazing! They give up another day to be with the children and once again demonstrate just how important the children's happiness and well-being are worth. The children may not recognise it at the time, but as a mother and a teacher, I recognise the immense value of occasions such as these that not only meet the Every Child Matters remit but go beyond it. The summer fair embraces each of the five ECM outcomes:

 "Be Healthy": *The children run around, play footy, climb the giant inflatable slide, throw balls at crockery and coconuts, dance and sing!*

 "Stay Safe": *They feel safe to run around in "their space" with parents happy to let them wander off and play.*

 "Enjoy and Achieve": *smiling faces abound, they have the best fun, and they achieve independence and a sense of belonging, taking part in games, winning a prize, and being part of a team.*

 "Make a Positive Contribution": *The children turn up, encourage their parents to attend, and part with their hard-earned cash; participate in events, help with preparations, design posters, help or run a stall, sell ice creams, and help clear up at the end.*

 "Achieve Economic Well-Being": *I'm not sure parents would agree on this point, as it is their purses that are often being emptied during the event! However, I do believe the children have a fantastic opportunity to learn the value of money; balancing the risk of winning and losing in games such as the tombola, deciding whether to spend their pound on the giant obstacle course or have nine thrilling chances to knock the coconut off the shy; learning about running a stall, being polite to their customers, calculating change, and explaining the rules of engagement and so on.*

These skills, and being part of a community experience, build trust and create feelings of belonging and safety. The fun-filled day brings opportunities for every child's personal development, enhancing his friendships and his relationships with teachers and with learning. The summer fair may seem like just a fundraising fun day out, and it is. But it also creates an opportunity for emotional literacy for the whole school too. When children perceive school as a place of fun, friendship, love, and laughter, they are more likely to want to come to school and learn.

The summer fair also lays the foundations for new children to enter the school feeling relaxed and familiar with the layout and environment. Children use many skills before and after the fair that are invaluable in life without even realising they are learning. How wonderful to be part of such a magnificent and worthwhile day out! What a genuinely fabulous way to celebrate the whole school community! It is these magical times that the children will remember fondly. It is the outrageous gunking extravaganza that will build rapport and respect. It is the laughter and the excitement that will bring graduates back to their primary school just to say hello to their favourite teachers and enjoy the community that was once their home during school hours.

I thank, honour, and take my hat off to every PTA member, helper, teacher (of course!), and child who works so hard to make an event (that many take for granted) happen year-in, year-out. It is your commitment to the school that contributes to the emotional health and well-being that continues to make a difference in young people's hearts and, most importantly, builds bridges to healthy, happy attitudes to learning. Thank you! Thank you! Thank you!

Now close your eyes and imagine your community without your school in it. Take a deep breath in and out and imagine your community without any schools in it. Notice how this feels: notice the gap, the hole, the emptiness. Explore the lack of centredness, the lack of energy, and the disconnectedness of the community. Where are the children? Where is the heart of the community now that the school is missing? Take another slow deep breath in and now place your school back in the picture. Feel how this feels. Notice the energy shift in your image; feel the children being drawn like a magnet to this place of belonging, fun and togetherness. Breathe and smile as you recognise the all-embracing nature of this picture, a community whole and complete. You make this possible!

What you Offer to the World!

When you are entrenched in the National Curriculum and drowning in more paperwork than you thought possible for one solitary teacher, it may be challenging to remember that you are laying foundations for our future leaders. It is you, yes little old you, doing her best to meet the demands of the ever-changing regime, coming up with exciting and stimulating new schemes of work that still tick all the Ofsted boxes. You are the starting block, the springboard that gives birth to our potential leaders. Remember this as you battle on with the tedious monotony of form filling and justifying every breath you take... Not only are you supporting a new generation of learners, you are laying foundations to inspire young people to be compassionate and tolerant. It is you, as part of your school, part of your community, and part of your society, who impacts the world through the way you connect with your children and mould their young minds and hearts into open, curious and understanding young people. Do not underestimate the influence you have and the value you offer to our world. You make a global difference.

Close your eyes and take a slow deep breath in. Slowly let it out, and as you do, imagine your classroom filled with your gorgeous, cheeky, challenging children all ready to learn a fabulous nugget from you. Take another deep breath and imagine at least one of these keen minds being so inspired by what you are saying, and how you are saying it, that it opens his mind to a depth you cannot comprehend. His heart bursts with inspiration, his mind connects with his heart, and his body responds with a tingling sensation that he remembers all his life. This magic moment is the catalyst of his dream to become a leader in the field of [...............](fill in the gap with the subject of your passion). Over time, and through sheer determination, fed by that first explosion of inspiration, he becomes a visionary in this field. Perhaps he makes a discovery that benefits humankind.. Because of your unique flavour of teaching, you touched his heart in an instant that not only changed his life forever but changed the course of history. Ready to acknowledge your value in the world now?

CHAPTER TWO

The Diamond Within

The Diamond Within

*"What we learn with pleasure
we never forget."*

Alfred Mercier

Teachers are the most valuable resource in Education. Teachers are just like diamonds. (Ok, so it sounds super cheesy, but suspend your disbelief for a moment, please and thank you!) You are a diamond! Not quite in the "Diamond Geezer" sense, although that too would work. I use the Diamond metaphor as one of the core teaching tools when working with children, young people and adults. I invite you to consider how a diamond is created and the qualities of a diamond. If you happen to be wearing one, stop and take a look. Observe how it looks and what it represents for you.

Before you read any further, before I give you my interpretation of *The Diamond Within*, I invite you to spend a few moments, a little while, contemplating the diamond. You do not need one in front of you, just imagine it. Close your eyes and notice what it looks like; observe its shape, its texture, and its qualities. Notice what happens when it catches the light; explore how many sides it has. To make it easier, imagine you are five years old, maybe a little younger, maybe a little older. You are being given a big beautiful diamond to hold for the first time. What do you see? Let your innocent eyes explore this thing of beauty as if you've never seen it before. What do you see and how does it make you feel? You may like to write it down.

The Diamond is a beautiful metaphor for who you really are. It epitomises the essence of who you are on the inside and the qualities that make you the magnificent human being that you are. So let's list the qualities you came up with and see if there are any more we can add.

Let's start with the obvious observations of a diamond: Remember we can use the language of a child to enjoy its simplicity...

- It is clear.
- It is beautiful.
- It is shiny.
- It is sparkly.
- It is precious.
- It is many-sided/multi-shaped.
- It is reflective.
- It is strong.
- It is colourful.
- It is expensive.
- It is unbreakable.

Now what if we turned each observation into a human quality? What happens to our understanding of the diamond?

It is clear. If you are clear in heart and mind, you can see clearly and your judgement isn't clouded. You are focused. You know where you are going and what end-result you want. You think clearly and behave accordingly. You are motivated by loving thoughts, and kind action follows. This is my definition of genuine clarity. This clarity brings you to Stillness. It is this Stillness that brings you to an awareness that is expansive and liberating. We shall explore this Stillness in-depth later.

It is beautiful. Yes you may look gorgeous, but let's go a little deeper than that! No matter what has happened to the body, either through illness, accident or abuse, you can be beautiful within. The nature of who you are is beauty itself. Your heart and mind are beautiful creations that go beyond logic or reason. Let this beauty reveal itself through your teaching.

It is shiny. If you shine with love and enthusiasm for your craft, your energy and light expand outward and shine on all you teach. Your eyes shine with excitement and enthusiasm for your subject and with joy for teaching. Your "shininess" draws in your learners like moths to a flame.

It is sparkly. You sparkle! You are radiant! Your sparkle glistens in your classroom and touches every heart and mind in your care. Your sparkly energy is contagious, and your teaching has a sparkly quality to it that is almost magical!

It is precious. You are the most precious commodity in your school, equal to the children themselves. Without you, there would be no education as we know it. Sure, we can sit each child in front of the Internet and say "go learn", but I wonder what would happen? You are what brings learning alive! It is your precious gift as an individual, as a teacher, a communicator and provider, that inspires young minds to spread their wings and fly to heights anew. This is the most precious gift to have, give and receive.

It is many-sided and multi-shaped. Okay, so we won't focus on the obvious joke here about shape! Yes, you gorgeous teachers come in all sorts of shapes and sizes, and you are beautiful in whatever form you take! Your teaching styles also appear in all manner of shapes and guises. You are multi-talented and offer many skills and personal resources that are unique to you. You have many sides, some of which are more appropriate in the classroom than others! All your sides will have their place. Sometimes you will need to be serious, sometimes you are silly; sometimes you will chose to be rigid, sometimes flexible; sometimes you will help and sometimes you will support by not helping. You get the picture... Your multi-faceted skill base and ability to discern what each child needs in each moment is what makes your multisided diamond so important and vital to learning.

It is reflective. You reflect the beauty and talent you see before you. You are the best mirror for which a child could ever wish. If you echo the awe and wonder in the experience of learning, your enthusiasm will be reflected in the eyes of your learners. Your light will ricochet throughout the classroom and touch the hearts and minds of your learners. You reflect your wisdom through your words, deeds and intentions.

It is strong. You are strong! You have to be! Depending on your classroom demographic and the needs of your children, you will need to have emotional resilience like no other. You will have to be strong enough to deal with the emotional demands of your students and the pressures of the teaching day. You will need to draw on your inner strength to guide you through the morass of ever-changing curriculum requirements and feel strong enough to cope with the multiple personalities in the staff room! You are strong enough to not only cope with the huge workload but also to manage the challenges of juggling home life with school life. You have the strength to survive the rigours of Ofsted and the frequent classroom observations. You are strong!

It is colourful. When the light of your sparkly self lands on your diamond, just like a prism, you reflect the rainbow of talent that you are! Your colourful personality shimmers throughout your classroom. Your teaching is a colourful range of techniques and methods that capture the imagination of your students. Your true colours shine through when you inspire them to break through their perceived limitations and achieve beyond their expectations. The variation of colour and tone you bring to your teaching is what makes you important to the world of education. Your selection of hues will radiate throughout your teaching style and your classroom management.

It is expensive. A child may comment on how expensive a diamond is. Turning this observation into a human quality, one can say your diamond within is valuable. You are valuable! As I said at the beginning of this section, you are the most valuable resource in education. Recognising your value is imperative to connecting with your diamond. Or, connecting with your diamond will be the key to recognising your value in education! (And in life.)

It is unbreakable. Diamonds, according to Wikipedia, are the strongest gemstones in the world. They can only be cut by another diamond. Translate 'unbreakable' into a human quality, and I venture to say you are indestructible! The essence of who you are cannot be destroyed. Without intending to challenge your beliefs, I simply offer the possibility that you carry on inspiring and influencing your students long after they have left your classroom, oftentimes long after they have left your school! Your memory and the memories you leave your students (hopefully they will be good ones!) will outlive your body and your presence in the establishment!

Other qualities of a diamond also include being:

- Unique
- Special
- A representation of love
- Pure

Every diamond is **unique**, just like you. You will offer your own unique flavour of teaching. You will support your students in your own way. I am not here to say what the right way is (although I do have some vibrant ideas on healthy ways to manage the stresses and pressures of teaching!). I simply offer you the possibility that your unique flavour will offer something that no other teacher can offer, just because it is you!

A diamond is **special**. How can I possibly quantify your specialness? It is beyond language. A student may be able to offer reasons why they love being in your class, but then there is always some intangible quality about you that defies definition! You are special and more importantly, you are special to the children and young people you teach. What you do and how you do it makes you special.

I may be stretching the metaphor here a little, but a diamond in Western culture is apparently a girl's best friend. When a girl receives a diamond, it is usually a token of love. A solitaire is the iconic expression of a declaration of love. **Love** must be at the heart of your teaching: the love of your subject, the love for your children, the love of your vocation. The purity of this love is a state of being which a Mindful teacher aims to radiate to all you connect with. Paraphrasing Kahlil Gibran, bread does not taste good if it is not made with love.

To complete the picture, a diamond is **pure**. It is clear and therefore also perceived as pure. Its value is measured by its purity. It is a perfect analogy for the human heart. My belief is that Mindful teachers have pure intentions when they enter the profession; their hearts are full of passion and clear intentions to provide a child with the best learning experience possible. This purity provides a strong foundation for effective teaching and learning. Your pure heart deserves nourishment and fulfilment just as much as your students do. Connect with your diamond within, and you will rest in this profound presence of purity.

Your diamond qualities will wake you up to your natural magnificence. When polished and *paid attention to*, they will revitalise your approach to teaching and will provide all the internal resources you require to teach from the heart. By recognising your "*Diamond Within*", you will be able to nurture yourself and connect with your internal resilience in a way that goes way beyond the thinking mind. By spending time connecting, revering, and honouring your diamond within, you will in time be able to recognise and honour the diamond within others. Not only does this make your life so much more loving, it makes your ability to communicate with compassion easier.

Furthermore, when you communicate to the Diamond part of another person, you speak directly to his or her heart. You look beyond the outer layers, beyond the labels, beyond the surface behaviour, beyond the personality, and beyond the ego. You recognise the beauty beneath these layers and connect with the heart - the heart of their heart.

Taking Down Your Armour

The invitation is to take down your armour in all forms (emotional, mental and physical) first, so that you can open to your diamond qualities, open your heart, and be willing to recognise *their* diamond. The power this generates is phenomenal; it brings your best qualities to the teaching arena. Actually, if you embrace the belief, it can change the way you communicate with everyone you know. It will shift your focus with your loved ones, especially if you have children of your own or a family member who tests your patience beyond reason! Your relationships will change forever when you look beyond their surface behaviour and become willing to notice that the behaviour may stem from a place of pain. When you go even deeper, you can be with their pain and not want to change or fix it. You can connect with their Diamond and love the part of them that is pristine, flawless, pure perfection - the part of them that is untouched by anything, the part that they arrived as when they were born, the part that cannot be hurt by outside forces. This is the philosophy I have embraced for many years, since embracing my "Journey", and it enables me to be with students that behave inappropriately in the classroom; it enables me to communicate with kids that are labelled deviants and help them see through diamond eyes instead. This is the philosophy that empowers me to address and hopefully release all judgement when I am with a challenging colleague, client or friend. And the ultimate test for me was to wake up to the diamond within every prisoner I teach, regardless of their crime, be it drug dealing, murder or rape.

This is the most profound tool I use with my students. Waking up a child, in fact waking any human being to the magnificence inside them, is the deepest honour and privilege another person can have. You can use this understanding in your teaching. It can be an unspoken device that can help you when you are dealing with a very challenging child or difficult situation. It can also be a very practical teaching tool during Personal, Social and Health Education (PSHE) sessions.

This book, however, is for you. It provides alternative ways to support *you* throughout your teaching day and teaching career. There are ways to explore the Diamond metaphor with your students which require sensitivity and a safe environment. This is one of the key teachings I provide during In-Service Education and Training (INSET) trainings. I highly recommend you experience this training prior to using this work independently, unless of course you have extensive experience in emotional health already. I am writing a teaching manual to support you to do this; this will be the best place to refer to after your training.

Now close your eyes, take three beautiful deep breaths and, as you exhale, release any negative beliefs that may be covering your diamond. Release any armour that may be protecting or shielding your diamond. Slow down your breathing as you bring all your attention to your diamond within. Focus on your diamond qualities and how these make you the beautiful, radiant teacher that you are today. (If you are feeling fed up, tired, jaded and demoralised, just turn your attention to the time when you were fresh and sparkly, maybe in the early days of your career.)

Notice the inner strength you have to continue your teaching path, even when there seem to be so many obstacles in your way. Notice the many talents you possess as you juggle the demands of the curriculum with the demands of your students and the demands of your home life. Notice how you shine when the students are with you; how you light up the classroom with your enthusiasm, even when you have a stack of reports to do and several meetings you could well do without this week! Observe your pure intention that is deep within you, driving you forward continually to improve the ways you teach, to develop your schemes of work, and to advance your lesson delivery. Feel how special you make each child feel, especially the ones that may be struggling with the topic or feeling weighed down by the pressures of their life outside school. Notice the unique qualities you bring to your students, giving them permission to be who they are and positively celebrating their uniqueness and achievements. Just soak in your diamond qualities and rest deeply, knowing yourself as this. This is your greatness. This is you in your greatness, at one with your greatness.

Remember how a diamond is created. It has taken time and a great deal of pressure for nature to give birth to it. Similarly, it may take time and sometimes extra pressure for you to recognise your diamond within. When you do, you will be liberated! You will celebrate your multi-talented self and all the beautiful qualities that make you who you are. Your natural beauty and inner sparkle will shine through to enable you to deliver dynamic and magical lessons that will inspire and motivate your students not only to learn but to be inspired to learn. Your diamond will be one of the reasons they want to go to school and will open them to the natural curiosity that may lay dormant. The pressure you experience in your teaching day may be the gift you need to help you recognise your strength and genius so that you can reflect your students' talent directly back to them!

Release any stale thinking around you and teaching. Breathe in fresh new ideas about how you can connect with your diamond qualities, and revitalise yourself and your Emotional Health curriculum. It's time to **reflect** on your magnificence, acknowledge your gifts, talents and beauty right now.

Realising the Huge Impact you Make...

One of my most significant personal achievements in my early years of teaching was at the end of my second year. I was working in an all-girl's comprehensive school with a generous range of ability. My Year-9 form had a handful of girls that were of high ability, but the majority were middle-to-low. It was in the days that Year-9 SATS (Statutory Assessment Tests) still existed. My girls had been dragged through the SATS mill, when most of them already knew exactly what their results would reveal. It was relentless and meaningless testing that simply reinforced their sense of inability. Many of the girls simply battled through, and more than a few rebelled through colourfully disruptive behaviour. They were lovely girls, however, doing their best to hide their achingly low self-esteem. Even the girls with higher than average ability were not blessed with very much confidence.

Throughout the year, I worked on breaking them out of the SATS mould. You don't need me to tell you the types of things we did to gently ease them into a place of confidence and self-respect. You know it's the little things: the informal times and chats; the discussions that go off the tutorial plan so that you can all get real and talk about the challenges that are beyond the paperwork; the fun times, sharing a laugh over crazy things that are going on in their world; and the hugs (that are now deemed impermissible) when they are dealing with devastation or disappointment.

At the end of the year, for Sports Day, we all dressed up in yellow (this being our house colour – sadly, it was the unspoken colour code for the "loser" house). I looked particularly ridiculous, crazy hairdo, bright yellow pompoms in hand, and lots of face paint spread over my features. After a great deal of persuasion, all the form looked equally as festive, and we had a blast that day. I gave the traditional rallying speech before we went out onto the field about taking part, being a part of something bigger, about living every moment to the full no matter what the outcome, and enjoying the moment to have fun and let go of expectations about winning or needing to win. It was a classic "let's-take-part-and-play-full-out" mindset. We sure did, and we celebrated the year with sunshine and sparkles that shone through our hearts, eyes and smiles.

I can't recall the final scores, though I don't suppose it was a first-place moment as we would have carved that into our memory banks! The point is, as I'm sure you recognise, that we didn't concern ourselves with the score. We had the best time participating, cheering, leaping about with encouraging gesticulations, and squawking at the top of our voices as the races ensued. Would it have been a "cherry on the top" moment, had we won? Sure, but that wasn't our main focus, and so we ended the day with as much joy and exhilaration as we had begun.

I describe that scene, not because it was particularly unusual but because it was, rather, part of the school experience. No matter what year a child is in, Sports Day is and should be a highlight in the school calendar for lots of reasons. One obvious reason is that it is an arena where the children can build their self-belief and recognise their value on and off the pitch/track. It is a place where encouragement abounds, and everyone comes together to support, no matter what. A little idealistic, maybe, but go with me on this one just for a moment longer. The spirit of the one who gives his heart to an activity, who, no matter what, keeps going and perseveres till the end; this is what you nurture. This is the magical energy that lights up the hearts and minds of the children and teachers in that moment.

I also recall a primary school swimming gala that my children were participating in. There was one race that literally took our breath away. Just like all the other races, it was one length of one stroke. The race began as usual, lots of cheering, shouting and encouragement. The young boys were steaming up the pool as best they could, and we all continued to clap and cheer as the winning boy touched the side.

The others followed up the rear with the exception of one boy. He was clearly not a strong swimmer. In fact, as he continued to splash and push his way up the pool, many of us wondered if he would make it to the end. More worrying still, he was thrashing towards the deep end. Our concern increased as all the other boys were finished and he was still floundering in his lane in the middle of the pool. The cheering lulled and the entire building hushed as all eyes focussed on a boy that seemingly had never swum the length of such a long pool. With each mighty splash the boy made, the audience grew more and more tense. Everyone was holding their breath. It was pin-drop silent except for his flailing arms crashing on the water. He paused, attempting to catch his breath (we all feared a lifeguard would be required); he attempted treading water in his own style and then began again. All the children, parents and teachers started to cheer him on, shouting words of encouragement, clapping as loud as they could, as if each clap might help him lift his arms out of the water to move him along. It was the slowest and most torturous length I had ever witnessed.

Eventually, this boy reached the deep end and grabbed the poolside. The entire building erupted. Everyone was on their feet cheering this incredible boy, who in the face of potential humiliation battled through the water to complete his challenge. He didn't come first, but he won the respect and support of every single person in that space. There weren't many dry-eyed mums, let me tell you. And even though he wasn't a boy I knew, just recalling this memory brings tears to my eyes.

This resilience, this strength, this determination had clearly been nurtured by someone in that boy's life. He not only did himself proud, he honoured every friend, parent and teacher that has ever encouraged a child to be his best and not give up. He represented every child that has pushed through his fear (whether it be with numbers, or letters, drawing, or sport) and grabbed hold of his courage with both hands (and in his case both feet too!) to complete his task. He was undoubtedly the champion of the gala. We were all bursting with pride and joy at this courageous boy's achievement.

These two examples will trigger lots more memories and examples in your own mind of times you have witnessed, and been part of, the acute joy and achievement that come through a child's ignition of self-belief. What I didn't mention about my class was that during the "end-of-year" assembly, they all stood up and shared their magic moments of that year. They all shared a similar thread. They each described moments of self-achievement, growing self-confidence, and blooming self-belief. They closed by thanking me for, most importantly, helping them believe in themselves.

Now that was a moment I will always treasure. They had begun to wake up to their own magnificence (whether they were academic or not). They not only recognised that I believed in them but that this had given birth to their own acknowledgment of their worth in the world. What better gift could a young woman give to another? So I thank these young ladies for giving me the opportunity to bring them to the mirror of life and to see themselves in it as the beauty and magnificence that they are. Thank you for having the courage and the willingness (with all the fear this brings) to look in the mirror and reflect your light. During a recent spring-clean, I stumbled across a copy of the speech they gave, here is an excerpt:

> *"...We did not know you for long, but what we know of you now, we love. You were always enthusiastic and you encouraged us to do our best, even if we did not succeed. You helped us through all the bad times and we thank you for that. You always had a smile on your face even though we knew you were having a bad day. You always had a lot of patience... You spoke to us as a friend, even though you were our teacher. We just would like to say thank you for all you have done for us all this year. You are the best form tutor and even though you'll be replaced with another form tutor, you'll never be replaced in our hearts. Thanks for everything... you made us believe in ourselves and we shall miss you.*
> From all the Assyrians 1. Goodbye and God bless you."

Nurturing self-belief is a delicate and finely tuned business. As I will discuss later in this book, each teacher and student is unique. Because of our unique qualities, each child, each student will require a unique recipe to build self-belief. The gifted Mindful/Heartful teacher will gently weave this unique recipe into each child's day. Some children may need a very stern hand and glaringly loud boundaries to rein them in; some will require a tenderness that they may never have experienced before to sneak in the back door of their self-worth; and many will require a cocktail of shaken and stirring techniques throughout the year. This is often done intuitively by the

Mindful teacher and through sound reflection of the child's needs. My experience is that the outward behaviour (especially in its raw, brash and uncontrolled forms) is hiding pain that they do not have the resources to manage, so they use the "hard man" strategy to keep outsiders from knowing what's really going on.

I was facilitating a Transition workshop for a Year-6 group and we were discussing the masks people wear. An extraordinarily profound conversation ensued. Many shared that they used their "happy" face to ensure they attracted friends and kept them even when they were feeling low. Many also wanted to please their teacher and "get it right" for her. It was deeply moving to hear just how connected they were with their feelings, and the willingness to share this with me was humbling. It was also a huge credit to their teacher, TA, and school, that they had the emotional language to share and the confidence to express themselves in the group. One would of course hope that by Year 6 all children would be comfortable to share, but this is not always the case.

The most memorable share came from a boy who was, on the outside, somewhat thrown together. The mask he talked about was heartbreaking, and I wondered afterwards: if this child had had the opportunity to explore and express this sooner, how different might his school experience have been. I so wished I could have given him some of the "tools" I was sharing with them then, earlier in his school life.

He openly and innocently shared that when he was feeling sad, upset or lonely, he would put on his "angry mask" to ensure no-one would come near him. He used a powerful strategy to keep his friends at bay to avoid feeling or addressing the pain. He was, of course, also subconsciously signalling a call for help to his teachers with his pain. A Mindful teacher will be aware of these unconscious (and sometimes conscious) strategies and approach each child and their behaviours with compassion and understanding. I know that when you are juggling a thousand and one other things in a day, sometimes you may choose, or feel you have no choice but, to let things go. The Mindful teacher will juggle the needs of each child with the needs of the class and her own needs as a teacher and a human being.

This is the challenge of the 21st-century teacher as educational demands intensify. In amongst the pressures, targets and deadlines, her core purpose is to teach, inspire self-belief and self-empowerment, and to ignite discovery and self-discovery through curiosity, passion and determination.

Taking time with each child; learning about his values, what makes his heart sing; inviting him out of his comfort zones; sometimes grilling him to ensure he achieves his best; bringing him to his heart; waking him up to his genius; helping him access his Stillness so that his creativity and talent can flow - these are what a Mindful teacher is all about. A teacher that bothers to do this sends the signal that a child understands. Words are not needed for the child to know that he is worth bothering about. Sometimes a student may need reminding (as I do regularly with my sons) just how fortunate he is that the teacher is giving her time on the athletics field or in rehearsals or for the maths challenge, all in her own time and not being paid for it. (If money is high on a child's agenda, he'll hear that one!). A great head teacher will effortlessly thread such awareness through assemblies and by connections with the children over time.

When a child realises that someone as important as his teacher is willing to help him, give him extra time, and create a little bit of magic for him (like a picnic party to celebrate the end of SATS), then hopefully he will know at some level that he is WORTH IT! What greater gift can you give a child? So keep on doing what you're doing and smile...

You may like to take a moment to sit still. Breathe deeply for several breaths and close your eyes when you are comfortable. Imagine a movie screen in the sky, and it is programmed with all the times you have built a child's self-esteem. When you are ready, turn on the screen in your mind's eye and watch all the memories of when you went that extra mile to support a child who was struggling, either with academics or with friendships or with troubles at home. Notice how you connected with each child, notice your heart softening and your mind opening as you explored ways to support and empower the child. Feel how you felt when each child embraced his challenge and, because of your encouragement and the inner strength you ignited in him, didn't give up.

Now take another slow deep breath in, and as you gently let it out, allow yourself a moment of recognition for the kindness you bestow on your students - kindness that not only builds their self-worth but also provides you with a deep sense of satisfaction and fulfilment. Soak in that fulfilment now. This is why you are a teacher. This is why you are a great teacher!

> *The Prosocial Classroom: Teacher Effects on Student and Classroom Outcomes* demonstrates there is *"growing recognition that teachers make a crucial contribution to the social and emotional development of the students* (Birch & Ladd 1998; Hamre & Pianta, 2001, 2006; Murray & Greenberg, 2000; Pianta, Hamre & Stuhlman, 2003) *that has lasting effects on their lives well into adulthood* (Pedeerson, Fatcher & Eaton, 1978). *Teachers influence their students not only by how and what they teach but also by how they relate, teach and model social and emotional constructs and manage the classroom".*
>
> Patricia A. Jennings & Mark T. Greenberg

The philosopher and speaker Dr. John Demartini talks about the natural law of polarity, explaining that there cannot be a negative without a positive. There is no such thing as a one-sided coin or a uni-polar magnet. Similarly, humans exhibit traits and their opposites: kindness and cruelty, passive and aggressive, helpful and unhelpful, etc. Children understand this implicitly, and as a Mindful teacher we can guide our wards to appreciate that it is safe to feel all our emotions, and that it is natural to feel both sides. Giving ourselves and our student's permission to feel happy and sad, joyful and raging, fearful and courageous, provides a forum to appreciate both sides, a balanced perspective. It also invites us to address the outside stuff by going inside, which is the key to my premise of teaching and learning from the inside-out!

Your behaviour can impact a child and the way that child feels about himself for a very long time. Your words, actions and non-actions can have a direct influence on a child's learning and self-esteem for many years to come.

> *"A child's life is like a piece of paper on which every person leaves a mark."*
>
> Chinese proverb.

Brandon Bays teaches how a situation, if felt during a heightened state, can literally be locked into the body at a cellular level. Her profound healing processes provide a means to gain direct access to that cellular memory and clear it out to enable healing and wholeness for the individual.

Just like every adult I have taught, I am sure you can vividly recall at least one teacher that had either a massively negative or massively positive impact on your life. They will have either boosted or crushed your confidence in a specific subject. Brandon herself recalls how her English teacher was so critical of her writing ability that she shut herself down to the possibility of ever becoming a writer. It was only when she addressed the pain through her transformational process that she was able to put pen to paper. She has now written several international bestselling books that have been translated into many languages.

Similarly, I recall being labeled an "average" student. In Year-7 English for example, I just couldn't get past the sticky seven-out-of-10 grade. I would spend hours drafting and rewriting and doing my best, only to gain a six or seven. But by implementing the Mindful techniques, I have since overcome the fear of writing and now rejoice in the ability to create this book.

I know I don't need to labour this point, but to give you a taste of what I mean, and therefore what we really want to avoid in the 21st-century classroom, here is an example. When I was nine years old, a teacher called me in to her Year-6 class, sat at the other end of the classroom, accused me of something I hadn't done, and shouted abuse at me in front of all the other children. This did not serve to boost my self-confidence and self-worth. I didn't have the resources to stand my ground, and part of me understood that it would not help my cause in that moment if I spoke up, so I kept quiet. My Year-2 teacher spent most of the lessons screaming at us to be quiet and smashing her wooden clogs on the desk to get us to "shut up!" This also didn't serve to develop my love of learning or build my self-worth!

Now, if we go back another generation, we can enjoy some really colourful tales. As I don't want this to be my focus, I'll leave it at that. But if you want some more juicy tales, just give my Dad a call and he will treat you to hours of torturous stories, especially of classroom punishments, that I pray would never happen today. And he's not even that old!

I truly believe and teach the premise that *no-one can make you feel anything.* (I know, easy to say, not so easy to embody.) It takes a deep exploration, perhaps some supportive training and a redirection of your perspective, to come to this understanding. Having said this, the above experiences - and I'm sure you have plenty more you could add - may well have triggered feelings in me of insecurity, lack of worth, and not-good-enough. From Dr. John Demartini's perspective, the mean and cruel behaviour may well have been the core driver to inspire you (me) to be the amazing teacher you are today. My painful struggle with low self-esteem has definitely been the fundamental motivator in my search for powerful techniques to help, support, and inspire young people to believe in their innate value and gifts.

On the other hand, I want to mention examples of the amazing positives that touch young hearts and stay with them forever. I have already mentioned three amazing teachers whom I will stay forever indebted to, but I would also like to mention the trainee teacher who taught an awesome and adventurous bridge-building project with us when I was 10. I can't profess to being particularly interested in bridges or engineering. However, I can vividly remember the thrill I gained from learning about suspension bridges by actually building one with straws! The energy in our classroom was electric. What we created was amazing. I think of this man whenever I cross a big bridge, recalling the awe and wonder he instilled in me that it was possible to work with the law of gravity and still create a huge bridge that could support itself. WOWEEE!!! (Big grin all over my face now) and that was 32 years ago!!!!!

I could mention so many more examples, positive and negative, but I'll leave you to share your stories in the staff room and around the dinner table. I must just close by honouring my primary school headmaster, Mr. Ryle. He was the epitome of perfect polarity. He had half-moon spectacles and a beard that gave him an air of authority and an expression that could match if the need arose. But he could turn into a cuddly bear who shared his favourite sweets with us (humbugs) on our first overnight adventure away from home. Approachable and scary, flexible and disciplined, warm and cool. Thank you Mr. Ryle, we loved you!

Nowadays, I have the pleasure to work with amazing 21st-century teachers who are inspirational, sensitive, and set clear boundaries. I bow to your patience and honour your commitment to your students. One of you inspired my geeky mathematician son to put pen to paper in Year 2 and come up with the funniest stories and the most amazing poetry. His work was genuinely funny, and as parents we had no idea he was capable of such creativity in this form. It was your flavour of teaching magic that enabled this! Incredible. Thank you!

So how about writing a letter to a teacher who made a positive impact in your life? Before you begin to write, close your eyes, enjoy three deep breaths, and take yourself back to the time when a teacher brought your heart and mind alive with the magic of learning. Breathe in the energy and feel how it felt. Feel your body glowing with excitement or wonder as you discover new things. Dive into the experience and feel the joy in your heart. Let this radiate out onto your thank you letter and speak from the heart. Even if you cannot track them down, the love and gratitude you feel will vibrate to them somehow, somewhere....

Here's one of mine:

> *St Peter & Paul's School*
> *Mitcham*
> *(1975)*
>
> *Dear Mrs. Vukojicic,*
>
> *Thank you for playing your guitar to us, for taking us down "the streets of London" with Ralph McTell and connecting us with our hearts through your beautiful music.*
>
> *I loved hearing you play and sing. I loved singing along and disappearing into my imagination and getting lost in the lyrics and the melody.*
>
> *Thank you for opening my heart through your creativity and for reminding me how lucky I was to have a home, a family and somewhere safe to sleep. I will always cherish the magic you created for me and my class.*
>
> *Love Kathryn x*

CHAPTER THREE

Take the Oxygen First!

Take the Oxygen First!

"What nobler employment, or more valuable to the state, than that of the man who instructs the rising generation."

Marcus Tullius Cicero

I'm sure you've heard the airplane analogy before - in an emergency, when the oxygen masks are released, put your own one on first. When I heard this with "parental ears" for the first time (as I was flying to the U.S. with my 9-month-old son), I recall being horrified the airline would suggest this. My instinct was to keep my son alive by helping him first! When I stopped and recognised the fundamental flaw in my thinking, I realised how often I put myself last for the supposed benefit of others, especially in my teaching. But how crazy to think I would be of any help to my students if I was "unconscious!"

Likewise, you are not much use to your students if you have not filled up with enough "oxygen" (rest/relaxation/fun/love/taking care of yourself....) What will you give them if you have nothing left in your own love tank? I know it's obvious, and yet with every "show of hands" I receive the same response: teachers put themselves last - limited loo breaks, going without lunch, too little water, early morning prep, late nights marking, limited social life, etc., etc....

There are hundreds of books about stress now. Many experts share mountains of advice on what to do and where to go for help. So in this chapter, I will briefly touch on the subject, but it's not my main focus. You're an intelligent reader and undoubtedly have experience of stressors and the symptoms they produce.

> *"Emotionally challenging situations such as maintaining discipline and teaching students who lack motivation are frequently experienced stressors for teachers."*
>
> (Hargreaves, 2000; Kyriacou, 2001; Sutton & Wheatley, 2003)

What I am interested in is the effect of long-term stress on your health and well-being, on your ability to function not only as a teacher but as a human being! I'm not interested in merely helping you to cope or function; I want you to thrive!

What if you could thrive in all you do? What if your teaching career inspired and fulfilled you so much that being in school and being outside school were equally fabulous, fun and fulfilling?

According to the Health & Safety Executive, stress is the second-most commonly reported type of work-related illness in the Self-reported Work-related Illness (SWI) questionnaire module included annually in the national Labour Force Survey (LFS). Teaching is among the top-five occupations affected by work-related stress, with 70% of teachers and lecturers saying their health has suffered because of their job. Further, female teachers (72%) are disproportionately affected compared to male teachers (66%). The health impact is even higher among school leaders and heads of department, with 75% and 73%, respectively, complaining. Thus, as the Teacher Support Network Survey (19th March, 2008) concludes: "Working in education is bad for your health and stress levels".

The National Union of Teachers argues their profession is *the* most stressful in the U.K., with mental illness on the rise. In the words of John Illingworth, a former primary head teacher from Nottingham who suffered a breakdown, "Depression, anxiety and burn-out have become the teacher's diseases, though they often remain hidden" (reported in *The Guardian*, 13th April, 2009). And The Samaritans report a suicide rate of 14.2 per 100,000 among the teacher population in England and Wales, compared with 10.25 per 100,000 among the general population.

In *The Blissful Brain*, Dr Shanida Nataraja reveals that stress-related disease has exploded as a result of ever-increasing pressures in our society. Heart disease, high blood pressure, depression and anxiety are at almost epidemic levels. Stress has also fueled higher levels of alcohol consumption, smoking, over-eating, and use of illicit drugs, while fostering a sedentary lifestyle.

Depression and mental-health disorders are also sky-rocketing. Even very conservative estimates suggest 15% of the population are clinically depressed. The true number, however, is likely to be much higher, as the diagnosis carries such a strong stigma that many do not seek help. The World Health Organisation (WHO) predicts that depression will be the second-leading cause of death by 2020.

Stress is a perception. When I was a child, there was no such conscious concept as stress. It certainly wasn't in my vocabulary, nor in the consciousness of primary-age school children as it is today. I still gasp when I hear my young sons say how stressed they are or that they have had a stressful day. You're 11! What could you possibly be stressed about?

But therein lies another book because, in their perception, what they are being asked to do in school *is* stressful to them! The demands on young people continue to grow, along with the negative labels imposed on them. Meanwhile, our society has lost the art of playing, and time for playfulness and creativity has been squeezed out of the curriculum. This has had a profound effect, not only on children, but on you, the teacher. And, as this book is all about you and for you, let's stay focussed on that! We shall address learner stress another day.

> *"Emotional stress and poor emotion management consistently rank as the primary reasons teachers become dissatisfied and leave teaching"*
>
> (Darling-Hammond, 2001; Montgomery & Rupp, 2005)

The Stress Management Society defines stress succinctly thus: "A situation where demands on a person exceed that person's resources or ability to cope".

This definition is clear and simple. The demands of 21st-century life are overwhelming. Juggling a full-time job with full-time family and social commitments is no mean feat! Then there are the unspoken expectations of how you "should" teach, how you "should" be a high earner; and how you "should" be ambitious and want to climb the success ladder. How many times have you been asked if you want to be Head of Department or offered promotion with lots of extra responsibilities, when in truth all you really want to do is teach? I am assuming that's why you entered the profession in the first place. I have met many head teachers and deputy heads who mourn their limited teaching time now that they are rarely available to do what they really love. What a shame!

Of course, many of you reading this may want to pursue the heady heights of senior leadership. That's great. I simply invite you to check what your motivation is and if it will serve your heart in the long term. If you do, fantastic! We need you! Enjoy the challenges and reach for the stars! So long as this brings you pleasure and satisfaction. If it doesn't, stop and take a look at what you love and what you would really love to spend your time doing. Take a look at *The Magicians Way* by William Whitecloud for inspiration. Darren Eden, himself a student of Whitecloud, runs workshops in the U.K. to guide you in unlocking your intuition and going for your heart. He gives you magical tools to help you focus on what you love. It's an awesome way to live!

In 2008, I founded Insideout Life with Sally Elias. Since then, we have been empowering teachers and young people to learn new ways to resource themselves from the inside out. If you know deep inside that no matter what happens on the outside, you have the resources to cope on the inside, you will be fine. Self resourcing is the key. As the Stress Management Society's definition reminds us, circumstances need not be overwhelming if we know what to do and how to manage the situation.

Anotole Francis says: *"Nine tenths of teaching is encouragement."* My job is to encourage you to explore ways in which you can reconnect with your inner wisdom, connect with your body wisdom, so that you can perceive things differently and respond healthily to potentially stressful situations.

> *"Unlike many other professions, teachers are constantly exposed to emotionally provocative situations and have limited options for self regulation when a situation provokes a strong emotional reaction. For example, when feeling highly aroused a teacher cannot simply excuse herself until she calms down. She has to stay in the classroom with her students. Indeed, coping with their own negative emotional responses is a major stressor for teachers."*
>
> (Carson, Templin, & Weiss, 2006; Montgomery & Rupp, 2005; Sutton, 2004)

I will give you practical techniques to manage the diverse range of challenges that life sometimes throws your way and how you can stay in charge of your thoughts and feelings, even in a crisis. My *Getting in The Right State* series is a training programme to support you and your students to learn and apply the methods so that you can connect with your inner skills and coping strategies during school hours and throughout your life.

What is stress?

Stress is an event plus the meaning you apply to the event.

> **Formula:** *Event + Meaning = Stress*
>
> **Example:** *An event occurs: I fail my exam. I place a meaning on this, I must be stupid. This generates a stress response.*

If we do not recognise a threat, we do not experience stress!

Therefore we can play with the definition...

Event + Meaning = RELAXED

> **Example:** *An event occurs: I fail my exam. I place a different meaning on this; I can do better than this. I choose to revise, apply myself, and re-sit. I believe I can achieve my goals. I relax.*

Some obvious stressors at school may include:

- ☹ *Ofsted inspections*
- ☹ *Paper work/emails*
- ☹ *New Government initiatives*
- ☹ *Lack of resources*
- ☹ *Curriculum demands*
- ☹ *Time restraints*
- ☹ *Scheduling issues*
- ☹ *Not enough space*
- ☹ *Financial constraints*
- ☹ *Challenging parents*
- ☹ *Children with behavioural issues*
- ☹ *Lack of management support*

Stress-related physiological symptoms may include:

- ☹ *Headaches*
- ☹ *Dizziness*
- ☹ *Fatigue*
- ☹ *Nausea*
- ☹ *Fast, shallow breathing*
- ☹ *Sweating*
- ☹ *Muscle tension*
- ☹ *Blushing*
- ☹ *Increased blood pressure*
- ☹ *Indigestion*
- ☹ *Dry mouth*
- ☹ *Diminished libido*
- ☹ *Reduced immune resistance*
- ☹ *Effects on the nervous system*
- ☹ *Effects on the digestive system*
- ☹ *Effects on the skeletal system*

The body responds to stress for a reason: headaches and dizziness are caused by the requirement for increased oxygen; as your lungs attempt to provide more oxygen, your breathing becomes fast and shallow; you can become breathless; blood pressure rises or you may experience palpitations as more blood is pumped around the body to carry more oxygen; saliva production is inhibited, hence your mouth goes dry; you sweat and blush more as your body tries to rebalance the extra heat caused by increased energy flow; your muscles tense up in preparation for an emergency, ready to leap into action; a build up of lactic acid can sometimes cause shaking too; the digestive system is halted, hence stomach upsets and nausea; and cortisol, a stress hormone, increases the likelihood of fat around the belly. (Dr. Marilyn Glenville has written a great book called *Fat around the Middle* if you would like to explore this further.)

But stating that stress is just a perception is enough to send anyone on the edge, over the edge. You are not imagining the heart palpitations or the rushing thoughts. You are not imagining the fast shallow breathing in your chest or the sweat pouring off your body. These responses are all real. What you need to look at is the thinking that preceded the physical reaction. Look at the definition again:

Event (Ofsted Inspection is announced at the staff meeting) + **Meaning** (What am I going to do? I only have one day to rewrite all my lesson plans, rearrange my classroom, change my displays, and tidy up the store cupboard... I'll never get it all done. And what if they fail me? And then everyone will know what a rubbish teacher I am and that I can't keep up with the paperwork and I'll be letting down my colleagues and my Head is so nice and I'll be letting down the children and I'll be so disappointed with myself and I'll have to leave before they sack me...) = **Stress**. Notice the crazy thoughts, feelings and beliefs that can take hold so easily and run amuck inside your head. And they travel much faster inside your head than they do when you're reading them, so imagine just how many more unhealthy and unhelpful thoughts can whiz through your mind, and that's before the meeting is even finished!

So the meaning you place on an event will have a direct impact on the level of stress you feel or don't feel about a situation. I met a Head Teacher at one of my INSET workshops earlier this year. She came up to me at the end of the training and told me that she simply didn't get stressed any more. Wow! "That's a big statement", I said. I asked her how, what her secret was, and offered her my job. It was very simple in her eyes. She had been teaching for a long time, and she would simply ask herself: "Is anyone going to die?" It's a powerful statement that brings all stressful thoughts to ground level! Great question!

Dr John Demartini states that *"the quality of your life depends on the quality of the questions you ask."* If this has resonated with you, you may like to close the book at this point and simply live from this perspective! It really is a fabulous question, and it worked for her. It may not work for you. So if you want to learn more about ways to address your stress, improve your life and your perception of it, read on!

> *"Remembering you are going to die is the best way to avoid the trap of thinking you have something to lose."*

Steve Jobs quoted in The Daily Telegraph, August 2011

How you perceive a situation is the key to how you react. Traffic, for example, may press your "buttons". It's often an unexpected disruption of your day. It may prevent you from getting where you want to go or in the timeframe you had anticipated. It can be perceived as an inordinate waste of time. Another perspective is that it may be an opportunity for quality time with a loved one or to catch up with a talking book, listen to an inspirational speaker, learn new methods to manage stress (but please don't listen to my relaxation CD whilst driving!), or ring a friend you've been meaning to catch up with for ages (on your 'hands-free' of course).

The possibilities are endless. I have a great friend who is particularly creative when it comes to traffic. She often has to drive at rush hour, and she is prepared for most eventualities. She even has a super cheap-rate phone provider programmed into her phone, so that she can ring family in Australia if she gets stuck in a jam. Traffic jams are an opportunity for her, not a misery, and she certainly doesn't waste her time.

I would like to add a few extras to her list of traffic-jam activities – one for the ladies (close your ears, men) that you can never do too much is pelvic exercises!! And you can practice the "Breath-and-Smile" technique (shared later) so that you arrive, no matter how late, unruffled, calm, relaxed, alert, and ready to perform at your best.

Powell describes stress as *"Frequent over arousal in response to **imagined**, **actual** or **anticipated** situations which we see as in some way threatening and which heavily tax or exceed our mental and physical resources to cope."*

This definition takes us to the nub of it. It is very similar to the Stress Management Society definition, but the most important clarification is in the words IMAGINED, ACTUAL or ANTICIPATED. This highlights the fact that our thoughts are dictating our stressed or non-stressed response. If you *imagine* the Ofsted Inspector entering your room, being highly critical of your environment, being rude and unsupportive and grading you poorly, this will trigger the same stress hormones in your brain-body as if it had *really* happened. Turn these thoughts into repetitive thoughts, and they become a broken record for the next three days prior to the inspection (or the next three months, depending on how much notice you've been given).

If this is your focus, you could seriously damage your mental, emotional and physical health by the time the inspection takes place. When a colleague ends up being absent for an inspection, it may well be due to her unconscious, self-induced stressors brought on by the very thoughts of the imagined events she was trying to avoid.

And finally we come to the...

Fight-or-Flight Syndrome

When a person experiences a shock or perceives a threat, the body releases hormones to help him or her survive. Adrenalin, noradrenalin, and cortisol help us run faster or fight harder...

"The fight or flight response was first noted by one of the early pioneers in stress research, Walter Cannon. In 1932 he established that when an organism experiences a shock or perceives a threat, it quickly releases hormones that help it to survive. In humans, as in other animals, these hormones help us to run faster and fight harder. They increase heart rate and blood pressure, delivering more oxygen and blood sugar to power important muscles. They increase sweating in an effort to cool these muscles, and help them stay efficient. They divert blood away from the skin to the core of our bodies, reducing blood loss if we are damaged.

As well as this, these hormones focus our attention on the threat, to the exclusion of everything else. All of this significantly improves our ability to survive life-threatening events. Life-threatening events are not the only ones to trigger this reaction. We experience it almost any time we come across something unexpected or something that frustrates our goals. When the threat is small, our response is small and we often do not notice it among the many other distractions of a stressful situation.

As well as this, these hormones focus our attention on the threat, to the exclusion of everything else. Breathing is accelerated to supply more oxygen for conversion to energy. The heart moves into overdrive to supply the body with more oxygen and nutrients. Our immune system is activated, ready to administer to wounds. Attention and sight become acute and highly focused and our sense of pain is diminished as the body releases analgesic hormones.

Unfortunately, mobilising the body for survival has negative consequences too. We are excitable, anxious, jumpy and irritable. This reduces our ability to work effectively. With trembling and a pounding heart, we can find it difficult to execute precise, controlled skills. Focusing on survival means we make decisions based on the good of ourselves rather than the good of the group. We shut out information from other sources and cannot make balanced decisions."

Stress Management Society

Fight-or-Flight reminds us that stress is not necessarily a bad thing. The imminent Ofsted inspection may be the perfect motivator to clear that pile of paperwork that has been weighing you down. It may be the perfect driver to get you to shine in your classroom, shake up your lesson plans, and become even more creative and imaginative. It may be the perfect time to polish your diamond and reveal that sparkle that may have been dormant this term.

Your students will want you to succeed. With rare exceptions, they feel personally invested in your success and will want to be a part of it. This inspection may be an unexpected gift to remind you how much your students respect you and are grateful for all that you do and the extra hours you put in. There will be a gift in the seemingly stressful situation. It's just a matter of shifting your perception of it and maybe looking at it from a new, healthy, wholesome perspective. Where do you want to put your focus: in the dirt or in the sky? Sometimes our heads plummet to the ground and it is a knee-jerk reaction to feel the gloom smother you as you hear the news, but you can do it differently. You can respond differently. You can be in charge of your state and change your state at will. (More about this when we talk about the weather in the next chapter.)

> *"Perhaps the most indispensable tool for man in modern times is the ability to remain calm in the midst of rapid and unsettling changes. The person who will survive the present age is the one which Kipling described as the one who can keep his head while all about are losing theirs. Unfreakability refers not to man's propensity for burying his head in the sand at the sight of danger but to see the true nature of what is happening around him and to respond appropriately. This requires a mind which is clear because it is calm."*
>
> W Timothy Gallwey, *The Inner Game of Tennis*

If You Don't Take Care of Yourself, Who's going to Take Care of the Kids?

We have established that stress can be good. It all depends on your perception and your perspective. Stress can improve your performance, keep you alert, and sharpen your focus. However, in the long term, chronic stress is not good for you. It will deplete your immune system, drain your adrenals until you suffer from adrenal fatigue, and can cause a multitude of fatigue symptoms that make it nigh on impossible to function, let alone teach or teach effectively. Stress can have a cumulative effect causing us to be excitable, jumpy, anxious, or irritable, or even lead to exhaustion and depression. This in turn reduces our ability to work effectively; we cannot perform precisely controlled activities and we struggle to make balanced decisions.

If you were to define stress in your own words, how might you describe it? It is helpful to spend a moment exploring how you actually experience stress. How it feels and how it shows up in your body. The more aware you are of your stressors and your reactions to them, the more able you will be to address them effectively. Give yourself a moment now to reflect on your 'stressometer'. 0 is calm, relaxed and groovy; 10 is off-the-chart volcanic. Examine a time when you are a little stressed, say at 2. What happens to your thoughts, feelings and actions? When you climb to 4, what changes? When you increase to 6 then 8, what escalates? By the time you reach 10, how are you dealing with the situation? How do you treat yourself and others? How are you communicating? Are you able to communicate with words, or does it become a primal sound? Let's let one out now shall we?

AAAAAAAGGGGGHHHHHHUUUUUUUURRRRRRGGGGGG. Lovely. That's better!

Here's my definition between 6 and 8: Everything is an emergency. I am on red alert and I can't think straight. My words get jumbled, I can't access vocabulary, and I can't express myself coherently. I don't know which way to turn or what to do first. I am snappy and shouty and am likely to cry at the littlest thing. Gosh I sound lovely! Does this sound familiar?

Just so you know that I'm serious about helping you take care of yourself so that you are able to do the job you love, for as long as you desire (and live the life you love), let me tell you a little story about a young woman who also loved to teach. She found herself teaching wherever she went, formally and informally; she just loved to teach. Whether it was fellow students at Uni, in theatre workshops, helping disabled adults rehabilitate after a stroke, or inspiring people with learning difficulties to build their self-confidence through drama, no matter where she was, she loved to help and she did this through teaching. She was a natural. She was invited to work in a secondary comprehensive and qualify on the job. Just like so many trainee teachers, she dived in head-first. Or should that be heart-first? She gave her all.

Her husband was very supportive of her and her incredibly long days. She would be in school by 7am and leave around 6pm, unless she was rehearsing when she could return home anytime up to 11pm. She would spend the evening marking and preparing for the next day. She ran the Art club, helped students with additional needs, co-directed the school performances, and stage managed the outdoor end-of-year production. She was deeply fulfilled and very happy. Admittedly, there wasn't much time for a social life or married life for that matter, but she was able to collapse in front of the telly with hubby on a Friday night.

The learning curve in mainstream education had been steep, and the constant proof and justification of everything she was doing was exhausting. She was working across three departments and didn't have her own room. So she spent much of her school day dashing around with stacks of books, whizzing along heaving corridors of girls, climbing stairs to her next lesson. Often her students arrived before her, which is such a no no! You know where this is leading.

Throughout her first year of teaching, she was in awe of her colleagues. How could they be so efficient, teach every day to this level, feel this exhausted, and yet still carry on? It turned out she was exceptionally exhausted. Her thyroid was plagued with tumours, and her adrenals were shot. By the end of her first year, she was very ill. Her body was burnt out. In fact she was so ill she was hospitalized. She had major surgery and missed her long awaited summer holidays plus the next half term of the new academic year. She was devastated. Interestingly, she had to learn the hard way, and because she was such a perfectionist and wanted to give her all to her students and her subject, she forgot to leave anything for herself! She knew she had to do it differently if she was to continue her vocation as a teacher. This enthusiastic novice teacher was of course me!

So let's examine some of the basics - fundamentals that are obvious and that you all know; commonsense stuff that you would say to your friends or colleagues if they were in a pickle, but that you don't necessarily apply to yourself!

 When you've had a break, you feel better.

 When you've had some fun, your happy tank is fuller and there's a willingness to dive into the next task. A lot less resentment arises.

 When you eat junk, you feel like rubbish after the initial high. When you eat nourishing foods and healthy drinks, you have more energy and your sugar levels remain balanced.

 When you've not had enough sleep or rest, you become irritable and a lot less tolerant of mistakes, mishaps, other people and their idiosyncrasies.

 When you spend quality time with your friends or family, your love tank is refueled, and you are more likely to be compassionate to others than if your love tank is empty.

You know what to do, but are you willing to give yourself permission to do it? When I am training teachers the Mindful way to teach, I ask them how many ever give themselves permission to have a break at break time or to take a full lunch. The pattern is unsurprising. There may be one or two members of staff in the entire school that give themselves a genuine break. I know what you're thinking. You need to spend this time preparing for the next lesson; you simply don't have time to sit down and eat your lunch Mindfully! I understand! I still find this one a genuine challenge. I didn't say what I had to teach you was easy, but some of it is really simple.

You will likely have heard the phrase Every Child Matters. I couldn't agree more, but what about the teachers? Here's a new acronym to add to your portfolio: ETM. Yes, Every Teacher Matters! Without you, as we have discussed, there would be no education community. Great head teachers understand this. The ones that book me to train and support their staff are the ones that understand they will eventually lose their staff either through ill health or mental or emotional burn-out if they do not take great care of them now! They remind their staff how important their well-being is, not only for themselves, but also for the healthy functioning of the school.

"The pressure which teachers undergo provokes physical and psychological pathologies to such an extent that the educative community is paying more attention to this problem which affects the quality of education"

(Sugar & Horner, 2001; Troman, 200; Woods & Carlyle, 2002),

"And work stress is connected to 50% of sick leave"

(Ponce et al., 2005)

Emotional Challenges

I've only touched on the practical aspects of teaching. I haven't begun to mention the enormous emotional challenges that teachers face on a day-to-day basis. Death, divorce, disagreements in the playground, fighting, friendship issues, children struggling with their ability or lack thereof, child protection, child abuse, child neglect. The list is endless. Teaching is emotionally draining. You need to be emotionally fit!

"Emotions may influence teachers' cognitive functioning and motivation, and students' misbehaviour often elicits distracting negative emotions that consequently can have a negative effect on teaching"

(Emmer, 1994, Emma & Stough, "001; International Labour Office, 1993)

In *The Prosocial Classroom: Teacher Social and Emotional Competence in Relation to Student and Classroom Outcomes*, Patricia Jennings and Mark Greenberg from Pennsylvania State University highlight the importance of teachers' social and emotional competence (SEC) and well-being in the development and maintenance of supportive teacher-student relationships and effective classroom management. Here follow pertinent findings on how emotionally fit (competent) teachers can support student well-being and improve the teaching and learning environment.

> *"Socially and emotionally competent teachers set the tone of the classroom by developing supportive and encouraging relationships with their students... establishing and implementing behavioural guidelines in ways that promote intrinsic motivation, coaching students through conflict situations, encouraging cooperation among students and acting as a role model for respectful and appropriate communication and exhibitions of prosocial behaviour.*
>
> *When teachers lack the resources to effectively manage the social and emotional challenges within the particular context of their school or classroom, children show lower levels of on-task behaviour and performance"*
>
> (Marzano, Marzano, & Pickering, 2003)

Emotionally exhausted teachers are at risk of becoming cynical and callous and may eventually drop out of the teaching workforce.

You need to be fit for the classroom, fit for the intellectual demands, fit for the physical demands (I rarely sit during a teaching day), and emotionally fit to manage the plethora of pulls on your heart each day – Tracy's Dad committing suicide, Bradley's Dad back in prison, Jack's Mum struggling with alcohol addiction, Susan's low self-worth, Craig's frustration with his inability to read, and the list goes on and on. And this doesn't include *your* real-life rollercoaster of dramas and crises that is the nature of being human: your kitchen ceiling falls down, your Mum is taken ill, your son is knocked off his bicycle, your friend dies unexpectedly, and your car window has been smashed. The list is endless.

In the immortal words of Forest Gump: "Life is like a box of chocolates, you just never know what you're gonna get". Staying with the chocolate analogy, life can be bitter and it can be sweet, and so is teaching. It is your responsibility to take good care of yourself. No-one's going to do it for you. You may have a terrific head teacher who encourages you to spend time relaxing in the staff room. You may have a fantastic family who support your vocation, make you dinner, and help you with the household chores. You may even have the most superb teaching assistant, but if you don't allow yourself time to breathe, or give yourself permission to relax, none of this will keep you standing, and you know you will not be doing the best you can. Then again, you may not even have any of this support, just many more demands, which is why it is even more important for you to stop and give yourself the oxygen first!

Jennings and Greenberg refer to teacher *"Burnout Cascade"*, when the classroom climate deteriorates to such a degree that teachers become emotionally exhausted as they attempt to manage increasingly troublesome behaviour from students.

> *"Under these conditions, teachers may resort to reactive and excessively punitive responses that do not teach self-regulation and may contribute to a self-sustaining cycle of classroom disruption."*
>
> (Osher et al 2007)

For now, please remember, you are doing the best you can with the resources you have at this time. So, no berating yourself if you are always first in and last out of the school building or if you don't give yourself permission to prioritise yourself and have a hot bubble bath instead of vacuuming the house or finishing some marking before bed. Hopefully by the end of this book, you will be inspired to do things differently.

Coping Strategies

So let's have a brief look at your coping strategies right now. A Mindful teacher will not judge what she sees, she will simply observe. However, she will be discerning. You will have a handsome list of strategies to cope with the challenges of teaching: some may be more helpful than others for your overall well-being; some may be the perfect antidote after a double lesson with 8E; some may be short-term, and some may be long-term strategies. However they show up, I invite you to explore your list now. You may want to write them down, or you may want to discuss them in the staff room. The top five that often show up when I ask the question during INSET is:

1. *Having a glass of wine (or three)*
2. *Eating, especially chocolate*
3. *Walking the dog*
4. *Spending time with friends*
5. *Having a warm bath*

There are lots more to choose from: smoking, socialising, dancing, TV, movies, music, hiding/retreating, reading, computer games, going to the gym, meditation, yoga, tai chi, spin classes, zumba, gardening... I'm sure you can add to the list. Depending on your perspective, some of these may be healthier than others. If you care about your physical health, you may choose ones that are body-focused; if you are more mind centred, you may choose ones that relax your thoughts; if you are an emotional type, you may choose a combination.

When being Mindful, you will let go of the label of positive or negative and simply observe what you do, when, how, and maybe even why. Your first really important step to becoming a Mindful teacher is to become AWARE. The more you are aware of yourself the more able you will be to observe and address your reactions and patterns of unhealthy behaviour. In time, you will be able to respond, rather than react, and release unhealthy patterns that no longer serve you or your students.

I invite you to become your best detective for a while. Set yourself a challenge. Treat it as a game and get really curious, just like Alice in Wonderland. Just for now, watch yourself and become an internal investigator. Inspect your habits, reflexes, knee-jerk reactions, your buttons, when they get pushed and by whom. Observe your highs and your lows, mentally, physically and emotionally. Watch your energy levels, your stressful thoughts, and the way you manage your time. Do all this without judgement! Good luck! And let me know what you discover!

My *Getting in The Right State* series is about finding balance and living in balance: balance in the classroom, balance in the staff room, balance in the home, balance with your family and, ultimately, balance inside yourself. The most important relationship you are ever going to have is the one with yourself. If your relationship with yourself is healthy, then your relationship with others inside and outside school will have more chance of being healthy too.

Close your eyes, take three slow deep breaths, and enjoy a moment to yourself. Find a comfortable position and allow your body to relax. Let everything go just for a moment. Give yourself permission to enjoy a moment of peace. If legions of thoughts come rushing in to remind you about all the things you should, could, would be doing, notice them and let them be there. Now bring all your attention to your breathing and watch the natural flow of breath move in and out. Beautiful. Now invite your mind to imagine how you would love to live your teaching life.

Be creative with your imaginings. If you could experience a healthy work/life balance what would it look like for you? What would you prioritise? What is on your love list? What would you love to do in the classroom and what would you love to do when you leave? Have fun exploring how you will have fun! Breathe deeply as your highest values are met, whether it's more quality time with loved ones or more dancing at night classes. Feel how it feels to follow your heart and give yourself permission to take great care of yourself. Notice how you feel, act and behave when your heart, mind and body needs are met. Breathe and smile deeply when you have a clear picture of how it could be. Know that because you can imagine it, it is now in consciousness and therefore it can become a reality. Make this your focus. Focus creates reality. You can start by starting right now. Make it a reality and know you have a choice in every moment.

The Basics

Before we dive headlong into the Mindful techniques that will change your life and your teaching life, it is imperative we address the basics first. You need to see what you are doing well and what you can address to get yourself fully back into balance. Taking good care of yourself is simple, but just like applying Mindful techniques to your life, it may not be as easy as it sounds. You know what to do, but doing it, or rather prioritising it, is often another matter. Part of the magnificence of most teachers, one of your most compelling qualities, is that you are caregivers. In my experience (with rare exceptions), this comes naturally to you. The care-giving may show up in lots of unique forms, just like your diamond qualities, but it remains one of your strongest unconscious drivers to be the best teacher you can be. For this reason, many teachers I work with rarely put themselves first: You may forgo lunch to prepare the next great lesson, or spend time supporting a child or colleague if they are having a rough time. You are more likely to stay late after school to reassure a parent that their son is doing just fine, that he just needs a little more time to settle in to his new school, and so on and so forth. You are terrific! You do what needs to be done to get the best from your kids and to give your best. In fact, I would venture that, in every moment, you always give everything you have to give. Even when you feel your teaching tank is empty, your tolerance tank is low, your creativity tank is at zero, you will squeeze something out of nothing to give your students the best you can.

This is breathtakingly amazing and what I most admire about teachers. You go the extra mile usually without hesitation. (I am not, of course, excluding other professionals, such as nurses and carers, who also give more than their nine-to-five. It is just that this book is about you, the teacher.)

The only problem with this approach is that (as I have found from my own experience) it can lead to physical or emotional burnout. This book is intended to support you to not only avoid burnout, but more importantly to find balance, so that you can love your teaching life and **have a life!**

> "When teachers lack the social and emotional competency to handle classroom challenges, they experience emotional stress. High levels of emotional stress can have an adverse effect on job performance and may eventually lead to burnout. Among teachers, burnout threatens teacher-student relationships, classroom management, and classroom climate".
>
> Jennings and Greenberg

> "Burnout results from a breakdown in coping ability over time and is viewed as having three dimensions: emotional exhaustion, depersonalisation, and feelings of a lack of personal accomplishment."
>
> (Maslach, Jackson, & Leiter 1997)

So let's get cracking. Forgive me if you feel I am teaching you to suck eggs, but sometimes you just need to hear it from an outside source for you to really take action and make healthy change. What would you say are the basics to taking good care of yourself? Break it into three categories to simplify your task: Mind, Body and Heart (encompassing feelings and spirit/energy). My invitation is to stay open and be Mindful of your responses. Just notice where you have resistance and where you have ease.

BODY
Movement

I avoid using the term *exercise* as it often has unhappy and rigid connotations of what you *should* be doing, not what you would love to be doing. Explore what you would love to do with your body. If you have physical restrictions, don't let that stop you. Work within them, love what you can do, and work towards what you'd really love to do. I love to dance. Do I dance as much as I'd love to? No, even though I know it makes me feel alive and fresh, free and happy, when I do. So why not do more of that? Moving your body will naturally release endorphins, happy hormones, which will help you feel great. You don't have to be a gym junkie to be fit and healthy. Dog-walking is a great way to fill your body with fresh air and stretch all the muscles, including your brain, to new heights. It opens your heart to the wonders of nature (so long as you are looking up and enjoying the view!). If you don't have a dog, borrow one! And if you can't do that, create an imaginary one. It's great fun and will ensure you go out in all weathers to clear out any stuck energy and stagnant thoughts.

I recently had the pleasure of attending a YES Group meeting in London, where Edwin Coppard was speaking.. He reminded his audience that we are meant to move our body. It is natural and instinctive. We are not meant to be stuck behind a desk all day (and this of course goes for kids too!) He got us to explore the four archetypes, connecting sound and movement with each. It was fascinating and so simple. His intention was to ignite our natural power. It truly energised the room. So do what you can to shift your body and make a change from static to ecstatic!

I feel obliged to mention the obvious benefits of keeping your body well oiled and finely tuned. Just like a car engine, if you don't give it a regular service, things will start to go wrong with it. Let's change that negative statement. If you take good care of your internal engine/ organs and keep your muscles finely tuned, supple and stretched, you will feel strong and healthy and able to take on the challenges of a physically demanding school day! Notice the difference? We'll address language later, but please be Mindful of your thoughts as we progress through this self-care section. You may have a tendency to be negative about healthy eating and exercise and alternative forms of relaxation, or just feel like I'm asking you to travel to the moon as you simply believe you don't have enough time to do it. Please hold on, read on; the bigger picture will eventually inspire you to make a healthy change.

You do not have to turn into Wonder Woman overnight (let's face it, you already are Wonder Woman!). You can simply choose *one* thing today. It may be your water intake. Start with something simple and achievable and this will inspire you to make further healthy changes that will enhance your health, wellness, and teaching.

I know you know the obvious benefits to moving your body, but sometimes it's good to reflect on just how fabulous energetic movement is for you. It will make you *feel* good. It will improve your bone density and strengthen your muscles. It will pump blood round your body with fresh new oxygen to supply all your organs with the supplies they need to stay functioning optimally, including your brain. It is likely to clear your mind and open you to inspirational thought or creative problem-solving just because you are energising and relaxing. You will really get into your body and get out of your head. This is especially beneficial if you are in a negative broken-record state or stressing about an impending task like reports, Parents' Evening, or being observed.

You can, of course, literally shake out the stress. I love Ilchee Lee's Brain Respiration Body Tapping technique, which serves to tap out all the stuck energy in the body. It really works, makes you feel great, moves anything that may have got stuck during the day, and brings a group together very well if you fancy trying it at the next staff meeting! I also love Jill R. Johnson's Oxycise. It energises your whole body, improves body function, and increases your metabolic rate. In 15 minutes you feel great.

Remember there are lots of options. Experiment and have fun!!! Try aqua aerobics (great if your knees prefer low impact), Zumba if you love to shake your booty, Spin if you love to sweat like a pig, tennis, ping pong (surprisingly demanding, especially if you have to keep picking the ball up when you miss a shot!), yoga, running (if you love to get out and about), circuits if you love to be pushed to the limit with clear boundaries, hill-walking, cycling, skipping, trampolining, and so much more. How lucky we are that we have so much choice and all these wonderful options to move our body! One of my personal favourites is just to play Frisbee, catch, and footy with my family all at the same time! Great for hand-eye co-ordination, great for quality-time bonding, great to move the body and work up a sweat on a Sunday morning for the whole family. It's a winner!

Your turn! Close your eyes, choose what you'd love, see yourself having loads of fun, and loving it. Find your trainers, swimming cozzi or dancing shoes and go for it! Experiment, be flexible in both senses of the word and let me know what you choose!

Nutrition

Nutrition is more important than you may think. I have struggled with my weight all my life, and so I thought food was just all about getting thin or getting fat. But in recent years, I have come to understand how food is so much more than that, and since being a teacher I have witnessed its powerful and often detrimental effect on learning. Having my own children sealed my beliefs on just how influential nutrition can be on mood and energy. This is where I want to focus. Your mood and your energy are everything in the classroom. I shall explore this in depth when we discuss how you "create the weather". For effective, fun, and productive teaching, your mood needs to be sunny and your energy needs to be high; this is our optimum aim. You have permission to be pooped at the end of the term, that's natural!

Here are some basics that I believe will help you keep your energy up and your mind-body healthy. You may have heard this before, but I write it with love and the best intention, so I hope it will resonate in a way that inspires you to make healthy change for life.

Eat breakfast! And more importantly, make time to eat breakfast Mindfully (this one I am still regularly challenged by, and I work hard to ensure I have enough time to eat slowly and Mindfully as I prepare my mind-body for the day ahead). Eat a high-protein breakfast and you're flying high. Chuck out those horrid cereals and dive into some healthy eggs! Eat protein at every meal and for every snack. Yes, protein is what your mind and your muscles need to keep you fuelled and fired up for the day.

Eat lunch! Same as breakfast. High protein, lots of yummy veggies, and take time to eat in awareness.

Eat dinner! Eat early and ensure you have protein and plenty of nutrient-rich greens, just like Grandma would insist!

Snacks! Yes you guessed it! High protein, please! Keep your insulin levels level, and *you* will stay on the level too!

Here's a slightly trickier challenge. Listen to your body and tune in to what it needs. If it needs a drink, give your lovely body some water. More about this in a mo. If your tummy is rumbling, you have left it too late to eat. When you provide regular re-fuelling, you avoid those sugar-craving energy slumps. Avoid going longer than three hours without refuelling. Just like a car, you risk dredging up yucky stuff from the bottom of the tank if you don't top up with fuel before the tank dial is on empty! Don't wait. Listen and administer regular healthy protein snacks as if they were medicine. Treat your body with respect. Honour it and you will be rewarded with the energy and vitality of which you've been dreaming.

Here are a few real basics, which are so fundamental I wonder about mentioning them at all. However, just to be on the safe side, here goes.

Reduce or Eliminate Sugar!

Sugar is a mind-altering drug and will affect the way you think, function, and behave. A prisoner once told me it works faster than heroine to alter your state! Now that's one to verify! And to top that with another radical statement, sugar should be banned from every school in the country. Thank heavens for the fabulous Jamie Oliver and his courage to speak out, take action and make significant change to the food provision in schools. Have you noticed just how bonkers some of your students can be after break or lunch? Yes, there are some variables to take into account, but hey I say sugar is the biggest and most negative influence on a child's behaviour in school (that can be controlled or monitored, unlike playground interaction). Sugar affects some people more than others, but kids with behaviour issues really need all the help they can get to stay balanced and stable, as do we. So let's give ourselves and them a fighting chance to stay in charge. Cut it out or cut it down as best you can.

Reduce or Eliminate Caffeine!

Just like sugar, some people have a greater tolerance to caffeine than others. Personally it doesn't suit my body at all. To find out if it supports your body, either visit a kinesiologist and receive muscle testing to see how it helps or hinders you, or remove caffeine from your system for at least a week and see what happens. If you are a heavy coffee drinker and know you rely on it to get you through the day, I do not recommend you experiment during a school week. Perhaps experiment during half term or when you know you won't have too many other demands on your system. You can go cold turkey or you can wean yourself off gently; the choice is yours. Either way, observe the response. You may be surprised how your body reacts. Removing toxins from your body may bring up some unpleasant side effects, physical or emotional, for a day or so, like a headache or nausea, but trust me; your body will thank you for clearing out the toxins that don't serve to support your body. You can do the same experiment for sugar. I gave up sugar (in all forms, including complex carbohydrates (eating no more than 8oz. of fruit daily)) for 365 days, and the difference in my body shape, my energy, and my skin was phenomenal! Start with cutting down and notice the difference.

Reduce or Eliminate Cigarettes!

I can hear all you smoking teachers telling me what to do with this one! The instinctive "Don't tell me what to do" knee-jerk response fires up, and then *you* light up! Okay, I will say no more. If you love to smoke, you will perceive more benefits than drawbacks. Your conscious mind knows it is not serving your brain or body to smoke; however your unconscious mind says otherwise. If you want to stop, seek support, and clear out your beautiful lungs. If you don't, you don't. I appreciate this one is off-limits for many.

Reduce or Eliminate Alcohol!

"An innocent glass of wine at the end of a school day is no big deal", I hear you say! "A little of what you fancy does you good!" Absolutely! You will undoubtedly have heard that red wine in moderation is deemed to have health benefits. It's all a matter of choice and what works for your body. If you want to be at peak performance in all aspects of your life, I would advise putting a cork in it! Your body will vibrate differently with alcohol in it, and your brain function is definitely altered. It will negatively influence your intuition, which you use every day in the classroom, whether you are aware of it or not. Alcohol is a depressant. Is this how you want to feel? Explore what your motivation is to have a drink. Be really honest with yourself. Is it because you are seeking comfort? Or because you feel you deserve a treat after a tough day? Is it for the sheer indulgence? Is it a way to dampen down your sadness or exhaustion? Just take a look *Mindfully*. Remember no judgement, just observe and then make a choice. Choose health ;0)

Keep it Simple!

It's not rocket science, but our rush-rush world can sometimes make it close to impossible to do the obvious. Make life easy for yourself. Prepare a whole pile of veggies or salad for the week or half week. If time is really tight, buy ready washed veggies and give yourself a break. If budget allows, hire in some help and get all your veggies prepared (and your house cleaned, maybe shirts ironed at the same time!). It will be like you have your own salad bar and healthy pic-n-mix ready for when you get home! You are worth the investment!

I am not a nutritionist, but have worked closely with several experts. If you want to learn more about keeping stress at bay through nutritional support, as I suggested earlier take a look at Marilyn Glenville's work. She has a sound, commonsense approach that is especially supportive of women and their progressive cycles of development and the challenges these may bring. If, like me, you have battled with your weight, there are many experts I recommend. One is Kevin Billet, CEO of *The Journey*®, who created a programme called "Stop the Food Fight". He helps you to get to the root cause of what may be triggering the emotional drivers behind eating (whether it's too little or too much). It has helped me enormously on my road to a balanced approach to healthy eating and healthy living; healthy mind, healthy body, healthy life. Yes, thank you! Whoever you choose to help you return your body to balance, be patient and remember you're worth the effort.

Water!

As a foetus you are 90% water. When you are born you are approximately 80% water. As an adult you are approximately 70% water. Your brain is 80% water. If I said nothing further, I hope these facts would be enough to encourage you to drink more water.

Water carries everything your body requires throughout your system. It is vital to your survival. At only 50% water, you would not survive. As I am not a scientist, I will not dazzle you with any more facts; just remember your brain, blood, bones, and skin all need hydrating. If you feel thirsty, you are already dehydrated. It is great that children are encouraged to drink water regularly throughout their school day. It supports efficient brain function and improves their ability to learn. Similarly, have a sipper bottle on your desk and drink from it regularly. It is vital you are hydrated and that your brain-body is in balance. If you want to learn more about the power of water, have a look at Masura Emoto's amazing photos of crystallized water and the effect negative and positive energy has on its formation. It will knock your socks off! More about this later.

Please don't underestimate the power of water. If you do nothing else when you put this book down, please make a decision to be Mindful of your water intake from now on. If your staffroom doesn't already have a filtered water machine, please encourage your head teacher to invest in one. If you are a head teacher, get on to it! It makes a difference. It also brings water into awareness and increases the likelihood of regular, effortless consumption! It says your teachers are worth it!

You may like to visualise your body being cleansed every time you enjoy a drink of water. Imagine the water gliding through your body with the intention to clear and cleanse your cells. Feel your body responding to the gift of water and allow the toxins to be swept clean from your body.

Ever since I learned in childhood about worldwide famine while watching *Newsround*, I have said thank you for the clean water that comes out of our taps. We take our clean water for granted, so how about honouring your good fortune by blessing the water as it enters your body and thanking it for supporting and nourishing your brain-body?

One final word: you are not drinking as much as you *think* you are. Since childhood, I have always had to be Mindful of my kidneys so, I was positively encouraged to drink large quantities of water as a child. This has held me in good stead for adult life. Nonetheless, it wasn't until I began recording my intake that I realised how I could easily let it slip. During my training courses, I share with you the water equation so that you can calculate exactly how much water your body needs, unique to you. Little and often is better than a pint here and there. Be Mindful and sip sip sip!

Rest

I used to believe rest was for wimps and old people! How wrong I was! The body needs time to repair itself and needs "down-time" in which to do it. Your body will thank you if you give it rest and recuperation. I'm not saying you have to stop in the middle of the afternoon and take a nap outside under a knitted blanket; what I am saying is start to listen to your body. It may be crying out for movement, or it may be in desperate need of a rest. If you feel like I did for years retorting "you've got to be kidding! When *exactly* do you expect me to have a rest? Have you seen my pile of marking?!!!" You may not believe it is feasible to take a break. Trust me if you dare, have a break! Diarise down-time.

Not that long ago, Sunday was a day of rest. It was enforced leisure. Now we have 24-7 shopping and the Internet, and there is always something we should be, could be doing in school or at home. Friends, family and children have such a demanding social life that before you know it you're booked up with activities for weeks on end. What if you were to consciously book in silent time? What if you were to create some space for yourself? What if you could use this time to be Mindful, measured and motionless? (Don't you just love alliteration!)

You could start with a 10-minute commitment and see how that feels. I challenge you to take a 10-minute quiet time just for the sheer pleasure of it. More on this when I discuss Mindful Moments.

Once again, I invite you to explore and understand the huge benefits of deep rest. Rest can be profoundly healing for both mind and body. Give yourself permission to steep in a restful state and notice the immediate benefits for your body.

Sleep

Many teachers and head teachers struggle with sleep. (Many children do too, and from an increasingly young age.) The mind is very busy, and its job is to keep you safe. It does a great job, even if it is to the detriment of your sleeping patterns. If you are stressed and are anxious about what's happening in school the next day or the next week or term, your brain will do what it can to help and protect you. Wakefulness at around 3am is a clear signal from your body that it is stressed and that it wants to keep you safe, so it suggests you'd best wake up, stay awake, be on red alert, and get on with whatever you need to get on with, before it's too late! Thank you body!

But sleep gives your body the opportunity to heal and repair itself. The liver begins this task at approximately 10.30pm. If you are still busying about, working your little socks off, your liver will keep taking care of your waking functions. It will lose its opportunity to do its valuable repair work that can only take place whilst you are at rest and sleeping.

Go to sleep. There is much debate as to how much sleep a person requires for optimum health. Only you know what is right for you! Listen to your body and tune in to what your body needs. It will be as unique as your fingerprints. Your needs will also change during the course of the seasons and are dependent on what activities you have been doing during the day. I have lots of top tips to get a great night's sleep. Blackout is the first great step to sleeping naturally. Support your melatonin levels and give your body the signal it requires to release sleepy hormones into your system. Turn off the telly and switch off the lights! Start with that, and I'll tell you more during training!

Relaxation

"The Highly relaxed mind can stretch more broadly and quickly than a tense one, just like a relaxed body."

Nick Bayliss, Rough Guide to Happiness

Relaxation is vital to both mind and body. To complete this section on the body, I simply encourage you to begin with observing where you hold tension in your body and what triggers its onset. Start to watch your body at specific times of the day. As soon as you are aware that you are tense (no matter what the reason), you then have the power to change it. You are back in charge and soon to be back in balance. For example, for years I used to wake up with screaming earache. I went to the doctors numerous times and started feeling like a complete hypochondriac. Every time I arrived clutching my ear, I would be sent away with a flea in it! "Your ears are beautiful" the Polish doctor would bellow. "There is nothing wrong with your ears!" I just couldn't understand it. I wasn't imagining the pain! Then one day, when I sheepishly shuffled back to the docs with the same complaint, I was seen by a trainee GP. I love trainees, they look with fresh eyes! He asked me if I ground my teeth. I was surprised at his question as I hadn't gone to him for toothache. You can guess the rest. I skipped off to the dentist and mentioned I may have TMJ Temporomandibular Joint (which I didn't pretend to understand). My dentist made me a guard for my teeth and hey presto, no more earache!

I had absolutely no idea I was a clencher! I don't grind much during the day, but when I'm tense I clench in my sleep. As soon as I became aware of this, I could take action and do something about it. I was back at choice. After learning of my unconscious tension, I consciously worked at releasing the tension in my jaw before bed, focussed on relaxing myself before sleeping, and cleared my head of any worries that might show up in my jaw when I was asleep. After a little self-training, I no longer needed my guard. I was back in balance. Now, if I wake up with a hint of earache I know that there are unaddressed issues niggling me. I will look at what is worrying me and take healthy action, physically and mentally, to alleviate the stress in my mind-body.

Your body will never lie. If it shows up with dis-ease, it is simply telling you it is not at ease. It is your job to understand what it is you feel uneasy about. Sometimes you may need a specialist to support you to uncover what is going on, especially with serious illness. As an accredited Journey Practitioner, I would highly recommend Brandon Bays' *The Journey*® as a means to help uncover the blocks that hold you back from health and vitality. You may find a different modality beneficial. Only you can know what feels right for you. You are worth the investment, so start listening and get clear.

Alongside understanding your body (Louise Hay's *Little Blue Book* is a great starter to shift your thinking and challenge your assumptions about your mind-body), I recommend you invest time to simply love and nurture your body. Help your body relax. Support your body with soothing activities. They don't need to cost the earth. You don't need to go to a spa once a week, although that may be a lovely staff outing!!! Give yourself time for a soothing hot bath with relaxing salts or luxurious bubbles. Create a soothing atmosphere an hour before bed so that you can really unwind - soft lighting, gentle music, and maybe a scented candle. Soothe all your senses and make this a ritual before bed or on the weekend, so that your body recognises that you love and cherish it. It will reward you! If you feel you just don't have time to do it, make time! Change your thinking, change your mind, and change your life!

MIND

When it comes to taking care of yourself, the mind is the place you really need to address first. If your mind is in alignment with your highest purpose, you have a smooth and easy path to your goals. If resistance shows up in any form, you will need to examine your thinking and understand what it is that may be blocking you from living in balance.

Mindfulness Meditation is an elegant key to unlocking unhealthy patterns and living in harmony with yourself and your environment. I shall explore this with you in depth later. For now, let's take a look at the simple ways you can support your mind and thus take great care of yourself.

Firstly I would recommend you give yourself some "head-space" every day. Give yourself 10 minutes a day just to be still, to rest your mind, and to give yourself the gift of quiet. If you gasp out loud when you think about how it would be possible to carve a 10-minute space for yourself when you have so much to do, then start with five minutes! Keep it simple, and make it easy for yourself. If you are a full-steam-ahead kinda gal first thing in the morning, like me, it may suit you better to have your quiet time later on in the day. If you know you will nod off if you sat still with your eyes closed in the afternoon or evening, then choose a morning slot before the whirlwind of the day begins. Do what works for you and make this a priority! In the morning, you may like to visualise your day and how smoothly it will flow. If you are anxious about a forthcoming event, you may like to ask a "mentor" or "helper" to smooth out your path (use any helper who fits with your belief system: God, guardian angel, wizard, super hero...). Visualise your day the way you want it to happen and feel how it feels when you achieve what you want to achieve. Your imagination will support your mind and invite your body to relax! In the evening, you may enjoy spending your 10 minutes of quiet saying thank you for the blessings of the day. You can list them in your head or enter your thank-yous in a Gratitude Journal every night.

This is a nurturing way to release the day. You can be grateful for the positive and negative things that have occurred so that you can go to sleep with a balanced perspective of your day. It is inspirational and vitally important that you appreciate not only the joyful, seemingly successful events and experiences, but also the challenges and the perceived obstacles. Both will bring you to a deeper understanding of yourself if you spend time being grateful for them. And yes, I do include the annoying colleague who always points out your mistakes, and I do include little Jonny who just can't stop talking. These people are beautiful gifts to help you be stronger and better teachers. If welcomed and embraced, these people will be your liberators and will ensure you live as the best person you can be. Alternatively, you can simply sit and observe your thoughts without attachment.

Another exceedingly helpful technique is to take down your armour, especially before bed or before an important conversation. This will support your mental, emotional, physical state. Listen to my CD and be guided by my words. This is an incredibly powerful creative visualisation that will relieve tension in the mind and body. It will bring you back to yourself so that you can uncover what is really present in your heart. We wear armour for a multitude of reasons; we wear it consciously and unconsciously. We may wear it as a signal of strength, as a warning to others to steer clear or to protect ourselves.

Energetic armour is a natural response to a threat. It can help to protect you on all levels - mental, physical, and emotional. In some instances, it will be entirely appropriate to put up your armour, especially if under physical attack. However, the trouble with armour is that you can be weighed down by it, especially if you wear it for prolonged periods of time.

Imagine, if you will, putting on a suit of armour. What does it feel like? Just close your eyes, take a moment, take a deep breath or two and imagine how your body feels wearing this armour. Imagine how your muscles, joints and skull feel. Notice how heavy it is and how restrictive your movement becomes. Notice just how dark it is inside, especially with your visor down. List in your mind (or on paper) all the words to describe how you feel wearing this armour, such as: heaviness, claustrophobia, trapped, weighed down, inflexible, tight, crushed, rigid and exhausted.

Now in your mind's eye, gently begin removing the armour piece by piece. Begin with the helmet and release all masks you wear and all the roles you play throughout your day – teacher, mother, sister, daughter, aunt, wife, partner, friend, colleague... Take off the helmet. Allow your head to soften and feel your brain gently expanding and "breathing", able to function without pressure. Allow the neck plate to release, inviting clear communication from your throat. Allow all the burdens on your shoulders to gently fall away. Take off the breastplate and the backplate, encouraging your heart to open and your lungs to breathe deeply and easily. Release the armour on your arms and legs, inviting flexibility, so that you are free to move easily and fluidly in any direction you choose. And finally, remove the gloves and boots. No need to "fight" anymore, and no need to "soldier on". Now imagine all the armour you've removed turning to dust! With a slow, deep, deep breath, blow all the dust out of the room. Let it go. Now just rest. Notice how light, soft, flexible and free you feel. Notice how your heart, mind and body are softening, relaxing, and returning to their natural state. Without the masks and veils, acknowledge your natural beauty and uncover the truth of who you really are without any facade.

Experience the liberation as all your veneers melt away. Notice how light, strong, and more powerful you are without the weight (of responsibility) pressing down on you. Breathe deeply and observe how easy it is for you to lift the muscles in your face. Turn your mouth upwards as you smile with gratitude, relief and happiness that you can recognise yourself, your true self.

Know that you have a choice whether to wear your suit of armour or not. Recognise there are benefits and drawbacks to both. The invitation is to become intensely **aware** of whether your armour is on or off, up or down (however you like to imagine it). When you are in awareness of your armour, its thickness and the frequency with which you wear it, then you can be at choice when, how, and if you want to let it go. The more aware you become, the more you experience living your life without armour; the more easily you can access your heart, your heart's desire, your vision of what you love, how you want to be in the world, and what you may want to contribute.

Enjoy experimenting with this Creative Visualisation. You may want to explore it in a safe environment at first before you expand it into your teaching life. If you are feeling "gung-ho" then just go for it and see if anyone notices the differences in you or your behaviour. Remember, no-one needs to know you are making this shift; it may simply be that you experience life and teaching in a whole new loving 'lighter' way. You may find you can communicate more effectively with your students and colleagues; you rediscover the passion for your subject or for teaching once again. You may simply fall in love with yourself and with life!

The magical thing about taking down your armour is that so much more of your light can be seen and shared. When you are all armoured up, your magnificent creative light cannot get out and is rarely seen at its brightest. Marianne Williamson's well known quote springs to mind...

"It is our light, not our darkness that most frightens us. We ask ourselves: who am I to be brilliant, gorgeous, talented, fabulous? Actually, who are you not to be?... And as we let our own light shine, we unconsciously give other people permission to do the same."

If this is a whole new concept for you, go gently in your experiment and have fun with it. Be like Alice in Wonderland and simply remain "curious" without judgement as you observe when, how, why your armour goes up and when you feel happy and safe to let it down. And let's be honest, it is a lot more fun without armour.

Ultimately, the simplest way to support your mind is to understand it. Step One is simply to love the mind. During one Journey process, when I was getting in a pickle and my mind was playing tricks with me, I was invited to give my mind a kiss, and from that moment on, I began to change my relationship with my mind. I stopped making it the enemy and started learning to love my mind. After all, its job is the most important job in the world. Its job is to keep you safe. So bless your mind, love it for what it is, your number-one protector. When you begin to understand and love your mind, you will be able to make peace with all those manic thoughts and start to let go of the stressful ones. They are, after all, simply thoughts, and as such they can come and go.

You can be in charge of your thoughts, and I don't mean in a harsh controlling way. You can observe what's moving through your mind and simply observe it. It is only when you get hooked by a thought and follow it that you can get stirred up, and then your body and heart will respond, sometimes negatively sometimes positively. It doesn't matter. You simply want to be in charge and in balance.

You may like to explore just how seriously you take your thoughts. One of my biggest hooks was that I would take myself far too seriously. I still have to keep myself in check, especially if I have a seminar to give or a document to write where I am earnest to get my point across, or when I am being challenged by something or someone and I feel I must get it right and deal with the situation "correctly". I have a powerful perfectionist belief! My number-one antidote to this is to always have a red nose handy!

Some people always like to have a bit of spare cash, some like to ensure they have their emergency lippy with them. Me, I endeavour to have a spongy red nose with me at all times. This way, I can ensure I don't take myself too seriously. Very important for teachers!!! Very important indeed that you let yourself off your 'inner-critic' hook. Very important that your students recognise your humanity and that they in turn give you permission (consciously or unconsciously) to be silly sometimes, to make mistakes (if you believe it's possible to make a mistake), to have fun, and not to take everything too seriously. Go on, take a risk, have some fun, be playful; by doing so you will give every other member of staff or member of your family permission to lighten up too and have some fun! Yippeeee! How much more creative would staff or department meetings be if everyone was wearing a red nose! The perfect leveller.

When you begin to watch your thoughts, master your thinking process, catch your negative thoughts, and challenge them (Byron Katie is the master of this – check out *The Work* on the Internet), then you will be on the path to freedom - mental, physical and emotional freedom. Yes, your body will respond to healthy thinking too. Remember you cannot feel a feeling without a thought first, so it is imperative you begin to watch your thoughts and understand the way you think and where your focus is. This will be your liberation. When you relax, you will open a doorway to access your thoughts. When you are tense, it is very hard to understand your thoughts and make peace with them.

Do not underestimate the power of relaxation. Step one in the road to *Getting in The Right State* for teaching and bringing yourself back to balance, is to relax! There are so many ways you can relax. You know what will work for you. Start with the body, and your mind will follow. The more you connect with your body and feel grounded, the less likely you are to get stuck in your mind. TOP TIP – Asking the question '*Why?*' takes you deeper in to the mind. Stay in your body and focus your relaxation there. As your body relaxes, so will your mind. Conversely, as you relax your mind, your body will follow. There is no right or wrong way with Mindful Awareness, just a way, the way, your way. Have fun, experiment, watch what works for you, and notice where resistance shows up. If it does, no need to chastise yourself, no need to be harsh or critical, simply love your resistance to death!

Take good care of yourself, in whatever manner serves and supports your mind and body. You are worth it, and it will make a huge difference in your well-being. Start with the little things. Make simple, small, manageable changes. Praise and reward yourself for making a healthy choice, for making a healthy change to love, and support who you are. You are worth it, and your mind, body and heart will appreciate your new approach. Your mind-body will feel valued and cared for. In turn, you will be in a much better state to value and care for those you teach and love.

> *"Teachers who experience burnout are less likely to demonstrate sympathy and caring to their students, have less tolerance for disruptive behaviour, and are less dedicated to their work"*
>
> (Farber & Miller, 1981)

If you are not comfortable with the label 'Mindful meditation', or you simply don't like it, don't use it. Call it stillness, quiet time, free time, or my time. Whatever works for you! It is imperative that you take care of yourself so that you can live a happy, balanced life, inside and outside school.

CHAPTER FOUR

You Create the Weather

You Create the Weather

"Life isn't about waiting for the storm to pass;
it is about learning to dance in the rain."

Anon

What does a child really want from you as a teacher?

Special-Needs-Millennium awards holder, Julie Lankester, undertook a research study in the summer of 2001 called *Padded Budgies* (long story!). This study explored the process of thinking and learning by examining recent research into the workings of the brain and the importance of creating the right state for learning. She also considered the emotional association of effective learning. One issue addressed was *what does a student look for in a great teacher?* She asked children across Key Stage 3 and Key Stage 4 what quality they wanted in a teacher more than any other.

Turn back the clock and ask yourself now, what did you love about being with your favourite teacher? What was it about her that made you want to get to her lesson or stay in her classroom after the bell had gone?

When I ask a room full of teachers this question, I always receive lots of heartfelt replies. Many get close, but few hit the nail on the head.

So let's list some of the qualities that may be dancing in your head right now:

What a child really wants from his teacher (in no particular order), is:		
☀ Safety	☀ Fun	☀ Gentle
☀ Kindness	☀ Clever	☀ Strong
☀ Being funny	☀ Organised	☀ Sensitive
☀ Fairness	☀ Can control the class	☀ Enthusiastic
☀ Generosity	☀ Sets boundaries	☀ Energetic
☀ Sensitivity	☀ Creative	☀ Available
☀ Discipline	☀ Calm	☀ Accessible
☀ Patience	☀ Welcoming	☀ Understanding
☀ Happiness	☀ Sense of humour	☀ Gives praise
☀ Silly/playful	☀ Knowledgeable	☀ Encouraging

Yes, all these qualities play a vital role in being an effective teacher and a learning magnet. But the number-one quality children look for in their teacher is that he or she is HAPPY! Yes that's it! That's all they really want!

Just stop and think about this for a moment. Really stop. Close this book and contemplate the implications this has for the way you teach and the way your students learn. Hmmmmm.

The implicit message underlying their desire for you to be happy is clear. The subconscious signal you send out to your students when you exude happiness will be something like this:

- *I am happy to be in my classroom*
- *I am happy to be with you (the children)*
- *I love my job!*
- *Learning is fun!*
- *You kids are worth it!*
- *You kids are worth my attention, my love and respect*
- *You are worth the effort*
- *I want to be here!*
- *Learning brings joy!*
- *Learning (and teaching) is worthwhile*
- *My kids are important!*

And so on.....

This is what your children experience without words when you walk into the classroom as a ray of sunshine.

Fantastic! Now you've got a reason outside yourself for taking care of yourself and ensuring you put yourself first, so that you can be in the **right state** for teaching. The children just want you to be happy! What if the most important thing you do for your students is to ensure you are in the right state for teaching them? What if you began to focus on creating sunshine in your heart so that you can create rays of inspiration in your classroom? The most important thing when you wake up before school is that you prepare yourself in a manner that brings you to a state of poise and presence so that you are in balance for the teaching day because your students relax and learn when you are happy (and when they are happy).

Close your eyes and take a moment to explore how you might be able to generate a state of genuine happiness for yourself in your classroom. I do mean genuine happiness, a state of balanced joy. You do not need to be swinging from the whiteboard with ecstasy; you want a genuine sense of happy well-being. A child can sniff out a fake smile at 30 paces. Be authentic with the way you are feeling. You know your children, and if you feel it is appropriate to share that you are feeling sad because your dog has just died or that a friend is very ill, you will know when this feels right. When you are fully present (Present Moment Awareness) with your students, the dramas of your life will fade as you give them your full attention, and you will return to a natural state of balanced joy.

If you are unconvinced and have lots of "yeah buts" in your head, such as

- ☹ *"Yeah but **you** try teaching my class after 3 days of continuous wet play"*
- ☹ *"Yeah but **you** try it when you know your Mum is dying!"*
- ☹ *"Yeah but **you** try it when you know you can't pay all the bills this month"*
- ☹ *"Yeah but I'm just too exhausted to smile anymore"*
- ☹ *"How can I be happy when…?" Fill in the blank with your unique dramas!*

I invite you to ask yourself where your focus is. Bring yourself to the present moment, right here, right now, in your classroom, with this great new topic you're starting, with your lovely or challenging students that have their idiosyncrasies that you love and potentially drive you potty. Bring yourself to this moment and be present with them for them. Ask yourself, what do I really want right now? What would you really love right now (and you must stay in your classroom for this!)? What can you really control right now? The only thing you can really be in charge of is your well-being, your emotional balance, and the way you respond to your outer circumstances. This is how you create the weather!

You have the power to create sunshine or rain. You can consciously choose to bring storm clouds or rays of sunshine into your classroom. Be aware of your mood. The more AWARE you are of your mood, the more you can take charge of your mind-body-heart signals to your students. Slow down! A rushing teacher is usually a stressed teacher on some level or another.

This is one of my biggest challenges in teaching, even now. I want to cram so much content and value into my teachings that I risk rushing. I want to do so much, achieve so much, and squeeze so much into every second I have with my students - be they children, young people, teachers, or prisoners - that it can be detrimental to the learners and to the quality of my teaching. SLOW DOWN!

Some of you are brilliant at this. You have a measured approach to your entire lesson, and all is well. Great! Keep doing this! If not, become aware of your pace and check if your delivery expectations are realistic for meaningful learning.

One of the training programmes I provide within the *Getting in The Right State* series is called ***Getting in The Right State for Teaching.*** When you are rushing, you are less likely to be in the right state for very much, never mind teaching. Have you ever tried to get into your car when it's raining and you're late and you need to get somewhere important? You use the wrong key; when you find the right one it will not go into the lock, then it jams, and meanwhile all your marking is getting soaked..... Slow down! I scarcely dare use the well-known fable, but ask yourself: which lives longer, the hare or the tortoise?!

The reality is that you may be going through a really tough time. The proverbial brown stuff may be hitting the fan, and it usually does in more ways than one. It doesn't rain but it pours and all that. If you are aware that you have brought your dark clouds into the classroom, you have the power to change state. You have the choice. Being a

Mindful teacher, you have the skills to shift your focus, move your attention from a lop-sided perspective to a more balanced view and move toward the sunshine in an instant. When your students witness your ability to do this, you give them permission to feel their feelings fully, express them in a healthy way, and then move on so that their behaviour doesn't spiral negatively downwards.

Another reality is that something tragic or frightening may have happened to affect the entire school. This is why it is vital you develop your personal emotional resilience. I remember being half way through training an INSET session with a fabulous group of teachers, when the deputy head interrupted the session to announce a young member of their staff had died. It was traumatic and a gift. We used the techniques I was teaching them to be present with their grief, and they all managed to not only stay in the room and complete the training, they also commented on just how helpful it was to deal with the unexpected crisis in that moment. One lady wrote a lovely thank you note expressing her gratitude for the practical tools and guidance that day. She shared how it had helped her acknowledge her grief, healthily address it, and remain at school and be fully present throughout the INSET training.

When you are confident that you can manage and deal with whatever comes up on the outside because you are strong and resourced on the inside, then you will provide a strong embrace for yourself, your students, and colleagues, no matter what the situation. You will have the inner resources to bring sunshine back to the situation. You cannot control nor change the storm, but you can generate a rainbow to brighten the day. You can bring yourself and your children back to balance. There will always be a gift in the rain. The flowers are always grateful for rain....

This may sound cheesy, gushing, and fluffy, but beneath the flowery words (which I love!) is a powerful premise: that *you* create the weather. You are at choice, and you can make the difference that may direct or redirect a young life toward his vision of greatness.

You Have the Power to Create Stormclouds, Sunshine or Rainbows.

A simple and practical way to help you generate sunshine, even when your personal clouds are hovering, is to keep your environment 'sunshiny'. The first step is, of course, to have an organised space, so that everything has its place. My experience of primary schools is that this is generally done very well. Work areas are clearly defined, and there is order and clarity in the classroom. A clear desk inspires a clear mind. Ensure there is no unnecessary clutter in your classroom (and yes I am aware space is usually very tight, and I may be asking for the moon with this one!). My observation is also that there is often a huge amount of visual stimulus in the classroom, which is wonderful, and I often drop into awe and wonder when I tour schools as the classrooms are filled with imaginative and hugely creative displays. The only problem is that there is rarely an empty space, or rather a space for emptiness.

Children benefit from space - clear, fresh, soft, empty space. It leaves room for their imagination. A few schools are now creating meditation spaces or quiet rooms (that are not libraries!). Deputy Head Teacher Kevin Hogston, of the Latchmere School, Kingston, has created a beautiful haven of peace called *The Blue Room*. The children love it, and it keeps the teachers in awareness of the significance of stillness and the power of peace and quiet.

My experience of secondary schools is that the working environment varies greatly, depending on the teacher and the school's provision. This is one to explore for yourself, quite simply because being ordered will help you manage the chaos on a practical level. It's all about balance. If you spend hours getting organised and keeping order rather than setting to work and completing tasks, then it will obviously be counterproductive!

The important thing to remember is that you have the power to change your state. Building your awareness muscle will provide the skills quickly to shift your state from dark and gloomy to light and clear. It only takes a moment, and it can be simply a matter of choice:

choosing a new outlook, a new perspective, and a new way of being in that moment. A quick and simple way I do this is to pop my red nose on. If I am feeling anxious about a task or can feel tension rising in my body for whatever reason, I dig out my red nose (always have one in your bag in case of emergencies) and, by the simple action of putting it on, it shifts my state. It instantly brings me out of the mental hysteria and into the light and airy. You try it. It can of course be a great way to shift the mood in your classroom if things are getting heavy and the students see that you are willing to lighten up, not take yourself too seriously, and make a fool out of yourself for the sake of the kids. It's a great leveller and keeps the stressful thoughts at bay. Give it a go! Other options are obvious like putting on some moving music, changing your physical position, shaking out tension, or simply straightening up and lifting your posture.

If you know you are responsible for bringing in thunderclouds, or if thunder has been the method you've chosen to shake up your class, then you have the power to shift the energy in the room and bring about a change in the weather. You can let it go, apologise if necessary, and move on. This not only builds respect, it reminds students that you too are human (an alien concept to many young people I know!), and also gives each child permission to stand down, apologise and move on to healthy behaviour if *their* thunder and lightning has crashed into the classroom!

> *"In a meta-analysis of more than 100 studies,* Marzano et al. (2003) *found that teachers who had high-quality relationships with their students had 31% fewer behaviour problems over the course of the year than teachers who did not."*

Another challenge is that tragedy may enter the school or your specific classroom. If there has been a loss of life or an accident, it is your job to reassure, reassure, reassure. As a Mindful teacher you will have the emotional capacity to be strong for the children and be strong enough to show your emotions. Be real with your kids. They will simply want to feel safe with their feelings. If you are 'real' with them, maybe sharing your sadness, it gives them permission to feel their feelings fully rather than stuffing them down or holding them in.

Leaving strong emotions to fester or cook is a recipe for disaster. The emotions will come up to be heard at some point, even if it is decades later. Give your children a chance to be healthy, well-rounded young people. Support and develop their emotional intelligence; it will be a valuable skill that helps them through the rollercoaster of life. Be willing to scrap part or all of the lesson (they won't be able to listen or concentrate anyway), shift the focus, and address the pain or confusion. It will be a valuable lesson if your children see how you value their emotional well-being. By being aware of the needs of the moment, you can support them in ways a lesson plan or a scheme of work could never describe. You will be doing this intuitively already, but as you develop your Mindful awareness you will be able to respond healthily to each new moment with fresh eyes and an open heart. The more you practise the art of making it okay for the children to experience their feelings and guide them to a place of acceptance and non-judgement, the more likely you are to generate a group of young people more able to manage their feelings and therefore manage and readjust their behaviour with little or no intervention. (I am not suggesting you become their therapist – just simply provide them with the space and permission to be fully present with their feelings and to express them if appropriate.)

A beautiful example of this is of a young boy with special needs who had participated in one of my sessions. His support worker reported to me that Samuel had got into a state first thing in the morning, as he couldn't achieve a particular task he had been set. Usually at this stage, he would wind himself up into such a frenzy that no more learning would occur for the rest of the day. However, his supportive TA reminded Samuel what he had learnt with me the previous day and gently asked him what he could do to help himself. He remembered what to do. Not only did he remember, he then took powerful action using a breathing technique to bring himself back to balance. He chose to reattempt the task and did so successfully. His TA was astonished and explained that she had *never* seen Samuel recover from an *episode* or take responsibility for realigning his state of being. As you can imagine, Samuel was thrilled with himself. What a sense of achievement! This is self-mastery in the making!

The key to this is time, and I appreciate it feels like time speeds up in school and that you are permanently sitting on an exam/deadline/targets time bomb. However, in times of challenge I invite you (and your class) to take time out (and it doesn't have to be hours, a few minutes may be enough). Stop. Be Still. Breathe! Use The Jar and follow your breath. Breathe and smile! Appeal to your senses. Put on some soothing music, freshen the room with aromatherapy oils, or shake out the tension with a wiggle session, a big stretch, or get some fresh air for five minutes. This will impact your lesson in a positive and healthy way. You and the children will be more productive and be able to concentrate more efficiently when you return to work.

Body Influence

Remember that your body posture will affect the way you feel and the way you teach. Be the best mirror for your students. They will respond to what they see. So let peace reign in your demeanour. Move with gentle confidence and allow your voice to be steady, clear and measured. If your spine is aligned, it will support your mind. If you are feeling weighed down by the pressures of the day, you are more likely to have heavy shoulders and sunken posture. Make a concerted effort to hold your body the way you would like to feel. Lift your head and torso up and allow your body to support you fully. This will encourage your lungs to enjoy their full capacity and you can enhance your relaxed state with optimal breathing. Shallow breathing will only serve to make you more jittery and unstable. Teach your students that the way they sit in their chair will have a profound effect on the way they feel and, just as importantly, the way they learn. They will be more able to access information and connect with their limbic brain if they are sitting upright. If you want to get an important point across, always stand. It will be easier for you to access the vocabulary you need to express yourself, and you will be able to communicate more effectively.

In one particularly challenging school I worked in, I was genuinely up against it. My classes were filled with on average 70/75% Special

Educational Needs (SENs), many with Behavioural, Emotional & Social Difficulties (BESD). The entire school ethos was in an unhealthy place. There was an extreme mix of teacher/student behaviour. After a while, once I had established myself – which took some "out of the box" thinking and additional behaviour-management training, I might add - I began to notice that many of the boys would return to my classroom at lunch or break and just hang out. Many of the boys didn't really know why they wanted to, they just did. Over time, they would gravitate to my room, sometimes talk, sometimes draw or doodle, sometimes just chat or chill. They had a place of refuge where they could be accepted and be still. They found a space where they could rest at a deep level (where this may not be possible at home). They were welcome! They could stop, be still and relax, be themselves, and feel safe in a place of non-judgement.

It was my intention to have a "light" classroom where, irrespective of daily visits from the police or fights and chaos in other parts of the school, I endeavoured to make my classroom a place of peace. The boys would take the mickey - "yeah, peace and love, Miss" - and that was fine. They got the message that my classroom was a sanctuary and a place of inspired creativity, and over time they welcomed this, and even if they didn't like my subject, they would willingly enter the room.

> *"There is a growing body of evidence that supportive student-teacher relationships play an important role in healthy school and classroom climate, students' connection to school, and desired student outcomes, both academic and social-emotional."*
>
> (Abbott et al., 1998; Darling-Hammond, Ancess & Ort, 2002; Gambone, Klem, & Connell, 2002; McNeely, Nonnemaker, & Blum, 2002; Osher et al., 2007.)

Close your eyes for a moment, breathe deeply, and reflect on your intention for your classroom. Is it filled with light? What other-than-conscious experience do you want to provide for your students? What energy do you want your room filled with? Take a little time to visualise what you want for yourself (it's your home during the day, after all) and what you want for your students. It may feel a bit odd to do this at first, but what if you filled your classroom with love and light first thing every morning? What if you consciously energised your room with the quality you want to work in, and inspire your students with, that day? Experience how you feel when you re-enter your room, knowing it is filled with your personal magic. And depending on your belief system, invite God, Love or Greatness into the room, if that feels right for you.

Teaching and learning are such a gift and such a privilege. The magical exchange between teacher and student should never be underestimated. Keep that magic fresh and alive with pure intention. Imagine how your students will respond (not necessarily in a conscious way). As you open your heart and fill your classroom with this loving creative energy, those who enter may sense the invitation to contribute theirs. So no matter what the challenges are on the 'outside', you create the weather on the inside – for yourself, your students, and inside your classroom. Choose sunshine, warmth, and a healthy glow of nourishing, enthusiastic encouragement. You will generate a much more productive and healthy learning environment.

CHAPTER FIVE

Understanding the Mind/Body Connection

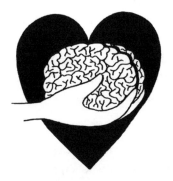

Understanding the Mind/Body Connection

"Health is a state of complete physical, mental and social well-being and not merely the absence of disease or infirmity."

World Health Organisation

Before you dive deeply into understanding Mindful Awareness, it is helpful to explore the mind/body connection. You may take it for granted that the mind-body is a unit or you may never have thought about it before. You may believe that when you are ill, it is because your body is broken, but my experience as a practitioner leads me to understand that the body shows up with symptoms because the mind-heart is sick. I have many examples where a person comes to see me because they are very ill, but when we get to the core issue, they have not addressed emotional pain.

One client had chronic fatigue, severe fibromyalgia, and a list of related symptoms. She was desperate, and the medical profession were flummoxed. She was a prisoner in her own body and she was housebound. She could no longer work and was very, very unhappy. When we began to explore the emotional root cause, she realised that her illness began soon after the death of her father. She had never allowed herself to fully grieve and had not come to terms with her father's death. In fact, she was downright furious that her father had deserted her when she needed him. When she began clearing this emotional pain, her symptoms began to ease and clear. "Modern research has shown that the condition of the mind has a direct impact on the condition of the body", Masaru Emoto, *The Hidden Messages in Water*.

Let me preface this chapter with a caveat. I am not a doctor nor am I a neurobiologist. I am a teacher, a speaker, and a practitioner. I write from a place of experience, not of scientific evidence (with the exception of quotes from other esteemed researchers). I offer you my instinctive, intuitive methods and years of self-observation and the observations of my clients. There is revolutionary evidence from many eminent Neuroscientists, such as Candace Pert, PhD, that link mind and body. In *Molecules of Emotion*, Pert explores how the chemicals inside us form a dynamic information network linking mind and body. "Pert's striking conclusion is that our emotions and biological components that establish the crucial link between mind and body offer a new scientific understanding of the power of our minds and our feelings to affect our health and well-being."

If you are curious about the science behind the work, please dive in and research away! If you are looking for a strong case for the effects of Mindful Awareness on the brain, look no further than Dr Shanida Nataraja's *The Blissful Brain*. Meanwhile, some extraordinary studies continue to emerge that specifically explore the effects of Mindfulness on teacher stress and to which I refer.

> *"Mindfulness-based interventions may be ideally suited to support the development of a mental set that is associated with effective classroom management... teachers reported significant reductions in emotional, behavioural, and gastronomic stress symptoms as measured by the Teacher Stress Inventory"*
>
> *(TSI; Pettigrew & Wolf, 1982)*

For the purposes of this book, I will touch on some of the scientific stuff, but it is not my field of expertise. If is far more important to me that I inspire you to take great care of yourself, that you are inspired to make healthy change, and that you become so motivated that you can't wait to practise! My number-one priority is that you do things slightly differently, Mindfully, heartfully, in your everyday life and in your teaching, so that you can inspire all the delicious young minds that have been blessed to be under your care and so that you can sustain your mind-body throughout your career, without the fear of burnout.

So, put simply, your mind, body and heart are not separate. When your body enters your classroom, you bring your mind and feelings with you too. When your students skip or saunter in, they don't pop their brains down on the desk and then leave; they bring with them their bodies too, with all their bumps and bruises, and they bring their emotional history too. You teach the entire "package" and you teach with *your* entire "package".

It's ludicrous that in school we focus almost exclusively on the brain part. True, true, in recent years the Healthy School Initiative is touching on physical well-being, and the PSHE Association has done sterling work for the past 20 years to build PSHE (Personal, Social Health & Economic Education) into the mainstream curriculum. And you, of course, are already a superbly awesome teacher, as I witness time and time again as you go above and beyond the call of duty to support and guide your students. Yes! Things *have* progressed. But there is still a huge way to go before emotional literacy and personal development are top, or at least high, on the school agenda. Why is it that in a place of learning, our children are not learning to take care of themselves at the deepest level? School, teaching, and learning are sacred! Let's make education heart-centred, and then the learning will take care of itself. The students will be balanced and hopefully happy and will have the emotional tools to link their lessons with their highest values. Kids will be skipping to school, not bunking off at the first opportunity!

Ask yourself a question. Right now, where is your mind? If I invite you to bring all your attention to your toes and focus just on your toes, where is your mind now? Interesting...

Ask yourself another question. How does your body feel right now? Stop, close your eyes, and explore how it feels. Is there any holding or tension? Are your muscles completely relaxed? Where do stress symptoms show up in your body? What does it look like? Does it show up as a frown, a headache, or an upset tummy? Do you have tightness in your shoulders or lower back? Is there an emotion in the physical tension? If there is, what is the feeling and where is it rising most strongly? Interesting questions, hey?

I believe in body wisdom. Ancient cultures, such as Native-American Indian, Maori, and Aboriginal peoples that are connected with nature intuitively know what to do when there is imbalance either of mind or body. What if you tuned into your innate body wisdom? What if you began to quiet the ego-mind so that you can hear your body whispering wisdom to you? My experience is that your body whispers to you all the time, you just may not be listening or want to listen. Sometimes your body will have to shout for you to wake up. In my experience, cancer is a great teacher and a powerful wake-up call for many people. What if you learnt practical skills to be able to listen inside so that you can support your mind-heart-body and avoid the challenge of an illness wake-up call?

A great question to ask yourself on a regular basis is "What's obvious?" Let's look at a fun example. If I invited you into a room full of delicious treats, everything from chocolate to aromatherapy treatments, how does your mind-heart-body respond? Just stop and take a moment to imagine it and then observe what you are thinking, how you are feeling, and what your body is doing (it may be a subtle response; it may not!). Now clear your mind and invite thoughts of a different scenario. This time, I am inviting you into a room full of creepy crawlies, creatures that give you the heebiejeebies. Once again, notice how your mind-heart-body responds! Is there a difference?

Similarly, you will have a noticeable contrast in response if I told you George Clooney (or the hunk/dreamboat of your choice) was waiting in the room to take you out for a date! And just so any male teachers reading this do not feel left out, imagine Angelina Jolie (or fill in the blank) is waiting for you! In case you prefer a same-sex relationship, mix and match as appropriate.

If, on the other hand, Mr. Bean or Nora Batty was your hot date, I'm guessing you may have a slightly different response. Yes, no? We take our instinctive intuitive responses for granted, but the fact is there is a natural pathway your mind-heart-body follows. In stressful situations, you will have a stressful thought first! Only after the stressful thought will you experience a change in the way your heart and body feel. Similarly, in a joyful situation, you will think a joyful thought first then the heart and body follow with happy hormones and relaxed muscles. The trick here is to catch the thought, hence the power of Mindful Awareness. The more aware you become of your thoughts, the more likely you are to recognise why you may be feeling blue or why you have a headache.

Your mind can support your heart-body or it can hinder it. If you were to spend all your time on negative thinking, it stands to reason that your body may become very tired, exhausted even. It may feel very heavy and tense. You are likely to feel pretty blue too. Never fear, it's not all doom and gloom! The reverse is equally possible. If you were to bring your focus to all that is balanced (notice I am not saying positive! – if you focus just on the positive your thinking will be just as lop-sided as if you were on the negative end of the spectrum), your body is likely to respond in a healthy manner, feeling light and relaxed.

There is another interesting twist to the mind-body connection. You can "trick" the mind! The phrase "fake it until you make it" is actually surprisingly helpful. If you hold your body upright, rolling your shoulders back and down, lift your chin a little to the sky, and maybe even walk with purpose, you will undoubtedly feel better! If you let your shoulders hang forward with your head drooping, you are far more likely to feel gloomy. Put your book down and give it a go. Or next time you're with your students get them to experiment and ask them how it feels to them! Tell your students there is a sound scientific reason why you tell them to sit up in their seats. It's not just so you can see which eyelids are up or down! If your spine is aligned you can access the limbic part of the brain more easily. This will enable you to connect with the emotional part of you that can get excited about the subject and communicate your learning more effectively. Make it easier for you and your students to learn. Get them to sit up or stand!! This will support and inspire their mind-brain heart-body to learn. So kindly sit up whilst you're reading my book! Okay, I'll make an exception for you; you can stay under the quilt for now.

If you want to change your state in one easy step, I mean super easy and super quick; simply shift your cheek muscles upward! Yes your brain will instantly trigger a relaxation response in the body if you **smile**. You don't even have to be happy. You can do a fabulously big Wallace and Grommit grin and hey presto, you are on your way to a happy balance! The Vietnamese Buddhist monk Thich Naht Hahn, respected author of *Peace is Every Step*, knows this only too well. He lives his life smiling on the outside and smiling on the inside.

> *"If in our daily life we can smile, if we can be peaceful and happy, not only we, but everyone will profit from it. This is the most basic kind of peace work."*
>
> Thich Naht Hahn

Smiling

Practising a simple smiling meditation every day will genuinely shift your well-being to being well. If you are feeling stressed out and anxious, simply bring all your attention to your breath. Close your eyes if it's safe (and appropriate) or keep them open (I do this often when I am driving). Take a deep breath in, and on the out breath, breathe out with a smile. It can be a super cheesy one or it can be a Mona Lisa smile; either way it will work. This is my favourite technique because you can do it anywhere at any time. Obviously you may get a few funny looks if you're at the supermarket checkout if you've gone for the Wallace grin, or you may just make someone's day brighter.

Your Mind Affects Your Body and Your Body Affects Your Mind

Remember, your subconscious mind does not clearly define or know the difference between real and imagined. When you wave your beloved off to work or your child off to school, if you imagine they will get there safe and sound, your mind-heart-body is in balance. If, however, you imagine they may be involved in an accident for example, my son *was* knocked off his bike on the way to school, your mind-heart-body will react to the thought unhealthily. Stress hormones such as adrenalin and cortisol will rush into your bloodstream, causing physical symptoms. Your heart may begin to race, your blood pressure may increase, your mouth may go dry, and you may even begin to shake just as I did when I got the phone call to say there had been a real accident. Now imagine what this will do to your mind-heart-body if you repeatedly think those thoughts every morning, day after day, month after month, when you wave your loved-ones goodbye! Not a balanced perspective. You will literally make yourself sick.

As a teacher, you can apply this to your working day: if you notice you are dreading going in to school, this is your invitation to stop, be still, and explore what it is that is dredging up these feelings. When you recognise what it is, when you are in full awareness, then you can take action, make a change to your situation, to your response to it, and where your focus is.

> *"Stress interferes with the ability to learn, it shuts down the brain"*

Professor Stixrud.

As a teacher or a student, you will impair your ability to learn or to retain information if your body is tense, if your mind is filled with rushing thoughts, or if your heart is aching and thereby distracting the mind from its learning task. It stands to reason that if a child is upset because of an altercation in the playground, he will be less likely to hear what you are saying to him. It isn't because he doesn't want to listen, it is because his stressful thoughts have taken hold and triggered strong emotions that inhibit his learning. His body is in the classroom, but he is not present. I'm sure you've been in a situation where you are perhaps at a party, you look like you are listening, but really you are churning over the events of the day or the bust-up you've just had with your partner. When my youngest was in his early primary-school years and I asked him what he had been doing that day, if he couldn't remember I could guarantee something unsavoury had occurred between his friends. It was as if he couldn't switch off the emotional mind-chatter after he had been involved in the upset. So no matter how fantastic the lesson was or how groovy the teacher was (and he had some fabulous teachers), he just couldn't hear them. He went on autopilot to survive the day whilst he wrestled with the troubles of his mind and the bruising of his heart.

You may already know lots about the brain. The more I teach, the more fascinated I become with this miraculous organ that most of us take for granted. Here are some Funky Brain Facts taken from Brain Health and Puzzles online.

- *Average dimensions of the adult brain: Width = 140 mm/5.5 in, Length = 167 mm/6.5 in, Height = 93 mm/3.6 in.*

- *How much does the human brain weigh? At birth, our brains weigh an average of 350g-400g (about 1 lb). In adulthood, the brain averages 1300-1400g (about 3 lbs).*

- *The composition of the brain = 77%-78% water, 10%-12% lipids, 8% protein, 1% carbs, 2% soluble organics, 1% inorganic salt.*

- *There are about 100 billion neurons in the human brain, the same number as stars in our galaxy. However, it has been suggested that there are more connections in the human brain than there are stars in the universe!*

The left hemisphere of the brain has 186 million more neurons than the right hemisphere.

750ml-1000ml of blood flows through the brain every minute (or about 3 full soda cans).

In that minute, the brain will consume 46cm³ (1/5 cup) of oxygen from that blood.

Of that oxygen consumed, 6% will be used by the brain's white matter and 94% by the grey matter.

The brain can stay alive for 4 to 6 minutes without oxygen. After that, cells begin to die.

The slowest speed at which information travels between neurons is 416 km/h or 260 mph, that's the same as today's supercar's top speed. (The Bugatti EB 16.4 Veyron clocked at 253 mph.)

During early pregnancy, the rate of neuron growth is 250,000 neurons a minute.

Your brain is about 2% of your total body weight but uses 20% of your body's energy.

The energy used by the brain is enough to light a 25-watt bulb.

More electrical impulses are generated in one day by a single human brain than by all the telephones in the world.

It is estimated that the human brain produces 70,000 thoughts on an average day!!!

After age 30, the brain shrinks a quarter of a percent (0.25%) in mass each year.

Albert Einstein's brain weighed 1,230 grams (2.71 lbs), significantly less than the human average of 1,300g to 1,400g (3 lbs).

One final gem: if every single person in the world had access to the Internet, the resulting network would still be only 1/15th of the average human brain.

As a non-neuroscientist, I shall just touch on the basics. In layman's terms, we have three brains. The neocortex, let's call it the modern brain; the limbic brain, often termed the reptilian brain; and the brain stem. The modern brain has been scientifically divided into all sorts of sections, and you can explore a brain map to discover where your language lobe lives and where your motor functions are controlled. A simplified explanation of the brain is that it has two hemispheres: the left for all things logical and the right for all things creative. The right hemisphere is where peace lives, so deep relaxation and Mindful Awareness will aid your ability to access your right brain. It follows that the more relaxed you are, the easier it is to teach and learn. Your ability to problem-solve and 'think outside the box' improves. The limbic brain in simple terms is the emotional centre. It's the ancient brain that instinctively knows how to protect itself and how to survive. The Fight-or-Flight mechanism lives here. It's your gut reaction. The brain stem looks after your basic functions and ensures your body ticks over properly, even when you are asleep.

Your 21st-century brain likes to think it's in control when it comes to decision making, but Dan Hill in *"Emotiononics"* suggests it is the limbic brain that makes the decisions emotionally and then the neocortex justifies the decision so that it can believe *it* is in charge! Contemplate for a moment, if you would, the consequences of this new understanding. We humans are strutting about the place with our super speedy technology and our high-tech gadgets believing we are the bees knees and have got it sorted, when in actual fact, when it comes to making important and possibly life-changing decisions, we revert to our reptilian instincts.

Now, no need to beat yourself up next time you reach for a packet of digestives or a glass of vino to deal with your stress. You know there is nothing logical about stuffing a packet of biscuits down your throat to ease the anxiety, but something drives you to do it anyway. This behaviour is not logical, it is emotive. It is the peculiar way your fearful, doubting, judgemental mind has chosen to keep you safe. It doesn't want you to feel uncomfortable, scared or unhappy; it wants you to survive and to feel safe. Your mind will tell you any story you like to ensure it does its job properly and keeps you alive.

Sounds a little counterintuitive, doesn't it? But this is what happens. It's not particularly helpful or healthy in many respects, but it keeps you alive!

The Gut Brain

There's another interesting twist to add to the mind-body connection conundrum. In a recent interview with Dan Hurley (*Psychology Today*, Nov 2011), Michael Gershon, Professor and Chair of Pathology and Cell Biology at Colombia University, explains that your *"gut works independently of any control by the brain in your head – it's functioning as a second brain. It's another independent centre of neural activity".* He goes on to say that *"the gut's brain, known technically as the Enteric Nervous System (ENS)...has an astonishing 100 million neurons – more than in the spinal cord but a lot fewer than in the brain – arrayed over an intricately folded surface area more than 100 times greater than that of your skin"* Dan Hurley notes that *"the ENS functions without any input from the brain. No other organ can do this. The ENS is the newest mind-body connection to be revealed. It also sends signals to the brain that directly affects feelings of sadness or stress, even influence memory, learning and decision-making. It relies on and in many cases manufactures, more than 30 neurotransmitters, including serotonin (happy hormone) that is identical to those in the brain".* Studies suggest the 'second brain' in our gut can significantly influence serious conditions such as depression and even autism.

Imagine this with me if you will. Things are getting pretty hairy at school. You've just had notification that Ofsted are due in, and so the headless chicken syndrome kicks in. Your workload feels like it's doubled, and there are still only 24 hours in the day. Your students are picking up on your tension and seem to be playing up more than usual. You are not handling it as well as you would normally; your colleagues are becoming snappy, irritable, and unhelpful; and the atmosphere in the staff room is stormy. Bam! You not only have a cold, you've lost your voice and your head feels like it is permanently crushed in a vice. A coincidence? In the last few days leading up to the inspection, half the staff don't even know if they'll make it through the teaching day. Any wonder that when the inspection finally arrives you are too weak to stand up, never mind teach?! How many healthy NQTs do you know at the end of their first year?! Did you know 80% of your immune system is located in your gut?

You know all about your gut instincts. I'm sure you could write a very colourful book about toe-curling teaching stories where you have not listened to your gut instincts about a teaching situation and the lesson has gone seriously pear-shaped, or when you "know" a child is on the edge and you haven't listened to your gut brain and intercepted the behaviour before he went AWOL. Next time your gut or any part of your body starts to jiggle, jangle or tremble, please stop, take a moment, observe, listen, and take gentle healthy action to support yourself, your mind, body, heart and class.

Creative Visualisation

Returning to the premise that your (subconscious) mind does not discern between what is real and what is imagined, you can use this to your advantage. For many years, Creative Visualisation has been recognised as a helpful way to support your mind-heart-body. Shakti Gawain describes in her book, *Creative Visualization*, the art of mental energy and affirmation and how this can contribute to physical healing and health. *"We contain the potential for everything within us".* The benefits of creative visualisation are vast. They have been employed by Olympic champions and world-class athletes for decades. The athlete that spends time on his mental attitude as well as his physical fitness is far more likely to touch the tape first than his counterpart who pays attention only to his body and not his emotional and mental health. If he believes, "sees" and "feels" the experience of winning every time he puts on his trainers, he increases his chances of crossing the finishing line first or wearing that gold medal. He is focused on his end-result!

Imagery in sport – also referred to as cognitive enactment or visualisation - is one of the most popular performance enhancements and rehabilitation techniques in sports. Dwight W. Kearns and Jane Grossman in *Perceptual and Motor Skills* (1992) examined the effects of a cognitive-intervention package, consisting of creative visualisation and relaxation on the free-throw shooting performance of basketball players. The results showed an increase in free-throw performance when employing mental training or mental rehearsal; players played better and scored more hoops. Researchers *(Feltz & Londers 1983, Mumford & Hall 1988, Ryan Blakeslee & Furst 1986, Suinn 1980)* have concluded that athletes who incorporate cognitive interventions such as visualisation and relaxation into their training programmes achieve higher performance than those who only train physically.

A gymnast will not only physically practice a complicated gymnastic manoeuvre – he or she will repeatedly rehearse the movement in his or her mind with mental images and movies of the sequence. The mental image/movie is continuously reinforced, much clearer and more readily accessible with every repetition.

If you believe you can make a difference in the lives of the young people you teach, and focus on this as your ultimate goal, you will, no matter how many obstacles. In fact, the greater the obstacles, the greater the drive and achievement when you touch the hearts you endeavour to inspire. Use your imagination to help, not hinder you, and positively encourage your students to do the same. I wasn't the number-one super-bright kid of the class, but I was able and I was hard working. Looking back, I gained my qualifications because I believed I could, and I put my thoughts into action every day by applying myself the way I knew best at that time. My thinking mind didn't entertain thoughts of failure (not for long anyway, even when I failed all but two of my mock 'O'-levels), because I believed I needed them to move toward the career I wanted. It was my intention to pass. I had no intention to fail. It was not an option! Had I known then what I know now, I would have spent a lot more time visualising myself holding my exam results and leaping about with joy and satisfaction, rather than worrying about what might happen if I failed!

Ask yourself what negative or destructive thoughts have crept in to your mind about your teaching that may not be helpful to you. The thoughts may be very sneaky and may only be a whisper, but they might be just enough to knock you off balance. If you stop, breathe, and take a look, you will be able to redress the balance and find your equilibrium once again. You may also like to explore Ilchee Lee's

'Brain-Respiration' techniques. You may enjoy learning about some more fascinating insights as to how the brain-body communicates and co-operates.

Brain Games

If all this brain talk and emotional exploration has made you feel a little weary, how about you have a little play now? There are lots of fun games you can play to challenge your left and right brain to work in harmony: try circling your right arm clockwise and your left arm anti-clockwise – simultaneously. And if you find that easy reverse it! Or you could play with coloured words that do not match the name of the colour. Read the colour, not the word, as fast as you can! Look up some visual illusions on the net, like the classic picture of an old lady and young woman.

There are some amazing ones that move too. It will blow your mind. Bring them into the staff room and your classroom and you will have hours of fun, and it will make you think twice about your assumptions about how your brain functions! Have fun!

Beta, Alpha, Theta

Before we close this chapter, it would be remiss of me not to mention brain waves. When we relax and become Mindful, we move from Beta (waking consciousness) to Alpha (relaxed wakefulness). When we deepen our state further, our brain waves move from Alpha to Theta (creative subconscious mind, imagination, dreaming sleep, deep meditation). From Theta, we move to Delta (very low frequency waves associated with the unconscious mind, sleep). These brain waves can be measured, and there have been many studies undertaken to measure the brain-wave patterns of Buddhist monks who have spent a life time in meditation, compared to the average person in the street. The benefits of meditation are numerous

♥ *Reduce your stress level*

♥ *Lower your blood pressure*

♥ *Lower cortisol*

♥ *Increase energy*

♥ *Increase endorphins*

♥ *Increase productivity*

♥ *Increase physical stamina*

♥ *Prevent or reverse heart disease*

♥ *Reduce pain*

♥ *Enhance your immune system*

♥ *Reduce irritability*

♥ *Reduce impatience*

♥ *Find creative solutions to problems*

♥ *Increase self-acceptance*

♥ *Reduce tendency to self-blame*

♥ *Increase acceptance of others and their idiosyncrasies*

♥ *Can improve inter-personal relationships*

♥ *Lower cholesterol levels*

♥ *Improve general well being*

♥ *Decrease need for sleep*

♥ *Decrease psychological stress*

♥ *Improve cognitive skills*

♥ *Gain personal insight*

♥ *Create greater capacity to express emotions*

♥ *Improve decision making*

♥ *Create a greater understanding of the bigger picture*

♥ *Reduce behavioural outbursts*

♥ *Improve and expand sense of identity*

♥ *Develop greater compassion*

♥ *Reduce alcohol and nicotine consumption (many male offenders choose to give up smoking during my Stress Management programme)*

♥ *Improve ability to maintain single-focused attention, even in the face of internal and external distractions*

It wouldn't take a rocket scientist to work out the beneficial correlation of Mindful practises with reduced stress, accelerated learning, improved teacher-student relationships, healthy classroom management, and improved teacher well-being.

A study of Mindfulness Based Stress Reduction (MBSR) for primary school teachers explored how stress within the teaching profession has a negative impact on the health and well-being of individual teachers and on retention and recruitment as a whole. In this small study, focussed on stress, depression, and anxiety within a self-selected sample of primary teachers, the results showed that most teachers were suffering from emotional distress, some of which was associated with self-reported impairments of motivation, self-confidence, and concentration.

> They surmised that
>
> *"benefits may accrue following Mindfulness training in terms of well-being, reduction in mental health difficulties, achievement of personally relevant goals, and enhanced ability to cope with the demands of teaching in a modern primary school."*
>
> (Gold, Smith, Hopper, Herne, Tansey & Hulland 2009)

To conclude this chapter, I invite you to go out of your mind!!! In her riveting presentation entitled *My Stroke of Insight*, neurobiologist Jill Bolte Taylor describes how she had the misfortune and the blessing to have a severe stroke. In a nutshell, her body shut down, and all she was left with was her right-brain activity. And there, she discovered transcendent peace. *"I felt enormous and expansive, like a genie just liberated from her bottle. And my spirit soared free like a great whale gliding through the sea of silent euphoria".* So profound was her experience that she wanted to share it with the world. Somehow she made the decision to leave the bliss and return to her mind-body, to heal, and to report her fascinating findings from the otherworld.

What if there was a way to access this bliss without the suffering? Brandon Bays, uncovered and developed a practical way to access this boundless awareness. William Whitecloud, too, in *The Magician's Way*, invites you to enter "Innocence" to connect with your intuition. Many other world teachers offer ways to experience the depth of who you are beyond your ego-mind. Mindful Meditation is a simple, gentle means to bring your awareness to the present moment. As you will discover in the next chapter, there is nothing but peace in the present moment!

Close your eyes, take three slow deep breaths, and bring your attention to this moment. Just be here, right here, right now. Nothing to do, nothing to get right, just be. If your mind gets chatting, simply bring it back to your breath and be still. That's all.

CHAPTER SIX

Mindful Moments Matter

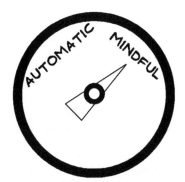

Mindful Moments Matter

"The future depends on what we do in the present."

Mahatma Gandhi

Jon Kabat-Zinn, Mindfulness teacher and bestselling author of *Full Catastrophe Living* and *Wherever You Go, There You Are,* provides a clear and simple access to Mindfulness Meditation. His definitions encapsulate the power of Mindfulness.

> *"Mindfulness means paying attention in a particular way: on purpose; in the present moment and non-judgementally. This kind of attention nurtures greater awareness, clarity and acceptance of present moment reality. It wakes us up to the fact that our lives unfold only in moments."*

'Mindfulness' is the translation of the ancient Indian word, 'Sati', meaning awareness, attention and remembering. **Awareness** brings you to the present moment so that you are conscious of it. **Attention** invites you to focus your awareness and train yourself to attend to this moment and this moment alone. **Remembering** keeps you awake to the possibility that you will forget! Being fully present in each moment can be hugely challenging, especially when living a 21st-century teaching life with all its mental, emotional and time-sensitive demands. You are re-mind-ed to remember and to stay awake to the moment, and be present with your learners.

> "Research indicates that contemplation and Mindfulness practices increase awareness of one's internal experience and promote reflection, self regulation, and caring for others."

(Ekman 2004)

To further quote the master, Mindfulness is the *"art of conscious living... It is simply a practical way to be more in touch with the fullness of your being through a systematic process of self-observation, self-inquiry, and Mindful action."* Jon Kabat-Zinn

Another term for Mindfulness is *Heartfulness*. This may resonate more easily with you, especially if you have not explored alternative ways to support yourself before. I enjoy both terms. Mindfulness invites you to be mind-ful, full of mind. This doesn't mean you go deeper into thinking and start asking tons of questions. If you do this, you'll only end up deeper in the ego-mind where judgement is lurking and ready to pounce! It simply means you employ your mind to be fully present to the moment. Heartfulness invites you to come from your heart. When you think, speak, and act from your heart, it is more likely to be expressed with love rather than anything else. Heartfulness breaks down the resentment, the inner critic, and victim mentality that can fester in the mind if left unchecked.

The Japanese character for Mindfulness is 念 It combines the words for "mind" and "heart" and elegantly captures the essence of Mindfulness as not just awareness, but awareness from the heart.

Mindfulness is simple. It really is what it says on the tin! It is simple, but not necessarily easy. It becomes easy when you stop arguing with reality (as Byron Katie, in *Loving What Is,* would say), and just accept what is in each moment. It is an invitation to surrender at the deepest level. When I use the word 'surrender', I do not mean giving up, as if you've been defeated, rather letting go. Letting go is often a genuine challenge, especially for teachers whose entire job revolves around being in charge, taking control, and getting things done. This is why it is so powerful for teachers, teaching and learning. It means that you can let go of life's burdens and responsibility that often weigh you down and prevent you from teaching in your natural flow and creative rhythm. It invites balance in your outlook and your actions.

> *"Mindfulness-based approaches are being recognised as effective ways to establish and maintain health and well-being."*
>
> (Baer2003; Brown and Ryan 2003; Williams et al. 2001)

You are a human being, not a human doing. In school, the pace of life speeds up. The timetable and the curriculum insist on everything being done in a certain timeframe. There is very little flexibility in this. While this structure can be helpful on many levels, it can also stifle creativity and leave very little room for inspiration and human beingness. Just being. What if you and your students had an assigned time every day to just be? How powerfully would this serve you and your students?! Imagine a flexible scheme of work that embedded self-inquiry time during the learning experience. Obviously, this may be more appropriate or more easily applied to some subjects than others, but you can imagine how significant it would be to the exploration of learning, self-understanding, and the motivation to learn, if you and the children were given just a little more space to breathe!

"We don't remember the days,
we remember the moments."

Cesare Pavese

Stopping, not doing, being, and surrendering to the moment, even if just for a little moment each lesson (and you can experiment when you and your students benefit most from embracing this) would, I believe, have a significant impact on your teaching and their learning. One of the most significant challenges you have is not necessarily getting your students into the classroom but actually getting them in the right state for learning. Being fully present (as opposed to mere "presenteeism" – being there in body but not in mind) plays a crucial role in learner progress. You may have 30 bodies in your classroom, but how many hearts and minds are truly with you?

Mindful techniques can swiftly and easily bring your awareness to this moment and support you and your students if they are "elsewhere".

The tragedy is that you can be the most spectacular teacher in the world; you can work your colourful little socks off day-in day-out; you can have the most inspirational scheme of work and exceptional lesson plans. But if a child is not *with you*, emotionally or mentally, you may as well be speaking alien. No matter how dynamic you are, if you do not have the practical tools to bring your children to the present moment, you are wasting your time because they cannot hear you, they are not there with you.

Imagine your mind is like a puppy. The puppy dog spots a squirrel and chases that; it spies a ball, it chases that; on the way to the ball it finds a bone, it starts to dig it up; and so on and so on. The same can be said of our minds: one thought dashes after another, bounces from one thing to another. As you know, you have the ability to leap from one thought to another and back again, especially if your list of things to do is growing fast that day. To learn how to manage your puppy dog mind will give you the awareness and skill to bring your children to the present moment. This way, you can enjoy teaching, as you know they are genuinely accessing learning and learning more effectively and efficiently. You sweep their imaginations along with you, and you are much more likely to keep them on task when practical challenges are set, like number-crunching or grammatical comprehension. You will be taking yourself and your kids off auto pilot.

The key to Mindful Awareness is peace in the present moment. There is no pain in the present moment. If we go back into the past, there may linger guilt, regret, and "should've, could've, didn't". If we push forward and take ourselves to the future, fear could strike at any moment with the dreaded "what if" mindset. Mindfulness is a place of non-judgement. You may think that it can play no useful part in teaching, as your job *is* to judge, critique, and improve your students, but the reverse is true. When you bring a Mindful appreciation into the classroom, the development and improvements you endeavour to teach will be experienced as loving guidance. Each child will ultimately be responsible for the way he responds to your help, but if you come from a pure intention to serve them to their highest, if you come from heartfulness, then your efforts are more likely to be received and acted upon with understanding.

There are obvious links between the qualities of a Mindful teacher and the characteristics of a socially and emotionally competent teacher (SEC). SEC teachers have very self-aware...

> *"They have a realistic understanding of their capabilities and recognise their emotional strengths and weaknesses. SEC teachers also have high social awareness... they are able to build strong and supportive relationships through mutual understanding and cooperation and can effectively negotiate solutions to conflict situations... They respect others and take responsibility for their decisions and actions... they know how to manage their emotions and their behaviour and also how to manage relationships with others. They can manage their behaviour even when emotionally aroused by challenging situations. They can regulate their emotions in healthy ways that facilitate positive classroom outcomes without compromising their health.... SEC is associated with well-being. When teachers experience mastery over these social and emotional challenges, teaching becomes more enjoyable, and they feel more efficacious"*
>
> (Goddard, Hoy, & Woolfolk Hoy, 2004)

I am not suggesting Mindfulness is the magic wand that can be waved once whereupon all challenging behaviour (yours and theirs!!!) stops. Just like any process, it is a journey. When I start working with an individual, I invite them to set their personal Sat Nav. I call mine the Kat Nav! Sat navs are so clever! If you programme in the exact postcode, you will arrive at the front door of your destination. If you put in half a postcode you will arrive somewhere in the region of your destination, but not the exact spot. Wouldn't it be great if you decided how you wanted to be and then programmed that into your heart? You don't need to know how to get there, only that this is where you'd love to be. Why not set yours now or, if you still need convincing that this way of being will help you exponentially, then return to this exercise when you've finished the book if you feel drawn to dive into the world of Mindfulness!

Close your eyes, take a few deep breaths, and get comfortable. Take your armour off, suspend expectation (of how you think this should look and feel), and bring yourself to the present moment. Open your heart and take time to soak into it. Rest here in the quiet and ask yourself what you really want for your life, inside and outside school. No need to go searching for answers; let them bubble up naturally.

> ## *"You are that which you are seeking."*
>
> St Francis

Ultimately, you may discover that the destination you programmed in was actually where you started. Home! Living a balanced life brings you home to your heart and brings harmony to the magical relationship between heart, body and mind.

Mindfulness takes time to cultivate and mature. You need to put in the practice. As Shamash Alidina states, in *Mindfulness for Dummies* (I am paraphrasing), you can read all the books in the world, study and gain degrees in Mindfulness, but it is meaningless without experiencing it. You will need to develop your own Mindfulness muscles! You can do this alongside your students in simple, gentle steps, or you can spend your high days and holidays learning, reading, and practising the art, so that you can apply it to your everyday living first.

When you experience Mindful awareness you will experience a subtle shift in your perception of all things. Just like your fingerprints, it will be unique to you and it will manifest uniquely every day. Your awareness will expand, and your perception of things may alter over time. My dream is that it enables you to live a balanced life; no matter how many times the government moves the goal posts or how many inspections you undergo!

The beauty about Mindful Awareness Practises (MAP) and Mindfulness Meditation is that they bring both you and your students into the human experience of learning.

"A view of human nature that ignores the power of emotions is sadly short sighted. The very name Homo sapiens, the thinking species, is misleading in the light of the new appreciation and vision of the place of emotions in our lives that science now offers. As we all know from experience, when it comes to shaping our decisions and our actions feelings count every bit as much – and often more – than thought. We have gone too far in emphasising the value and import of the purely rational – of what IQ measures – in human life. Intelligence can come to nothing when emotions hold sway."

Daniel Goldman – 'Emotional Intelligence,
Why It Can Matter More Than IQ' – 1995.

The trouble with our education system is that it functions as if it were a computer. The system is the hard drive, you are the software, and the kids have to plug themselves in as if they were a memory stick and then download the information. The problem with this model is that the memory stick has emotional filters when they are learning. Nothing will be successfully downloaded if the emotional filters are on high or when they see, feel, or believe there is no relevance in the information to their life. Their value filters are deeply embedded in their emotional filters and will not allow access, either consciously or unconsciously, if it is not meaningful.

Kate Hopkinson, consultant and founder of Inner Skills, has spent many years researching the patterns of inner-skill use that are rewarded, ignored, or punished in different contexts. The evidence points to children in the education system being rewarded primarily for listening obediently, setting work out neatly and in the prescribed manner, getting facts right, and doing what they are told – i.e., converging on the 'correct' answers and behaviour.

But engagement with, and excitement in, learning are associated with divergent inner skills, which involve exploring, challenging, rattling and shaking, and generally doing the opposite of currently valued behaviour: which may be why so many children disengage and can't see the relevance to themselves of what they are "learning".

More information on Kate's innovative methodology, called Landscape of the Mind, can be found at www.innerskills.co.uk.

Kate is also a senior research associate with the Complexity Research Programme at the London School of Economics (LSE), and there is information about her work on the LSE website at www.lse.ac.uk/complexity.

Given the desirability of SEC characteristics, isn't it extraordinary that little attention has been paid to supporting teachers, either during teacher training or through in-service training?

> "Given the very high demands placed on teachers, it is surprising that they rarely receive specific training to address the importance of social and emotional issues in the classroom or how to develop the SEC to successfully handle them." (Hargreaves, 1998).

You will of course recognise that you too will be teaching with emotional filters in place and are unequivocally affected by emotional personal history that enters the classroom with you in your DNA! The institution as a whole would benefit by becoming far more holistic. I am not suggesting we pander to all the emotional states of you or your students, but I am inviting an awareness of this and adoption of some healthy mechanisms to ensure every member of the classroom is in the right state for teaching and learning.

Becoming the humble observer in non-judgement, even just for a moment each day, will be the starting point for a whole new perspective of teaching and learning and your approach to life. The benefits are far-reaching, especially if applied to your everyday life as well as your teaching life. As you build your self-awareness muscles, you will inevitably become more emotionally fit as you observe your stress buttons and begin gently and non-judgementally to address them. It is often easier to receive help and guidance to do this, or at least to have a Mindful buddy to keep you "remembering" to check in and to understand from the heart what might be driving certain behaviours. Or you can simply stay focused on your "Greatness" and teach from this place.

As you develop your Mindful practise, even if it is a simple decision to slow down, you may not be able to put your finger on it at first, but there will be a sensation of feeling lighter around issues that ordinarily pressed your buttons. You will develop the ability to deal with difficult emotions for yourself and your students, just by being with them and not trying to "fix" the situation. Your self-observation will increase, not your inner critic. You are more likely to ask the question "What's the most loving thing I can do for myself right now?" You will be your own best friend, rather than beating yourself up and criticising your feelings of overwhelm or inability to tick all the boxes that day. You can simply turn down the volume on all this unnecessary noise. In time, this self observation will lead to Mindful Action. You may begin to recognise that your water intake is minimal and begin to bring regular drinking into your awareness and then take action by keeping a bottle of water on your desk to sip during lessons. You may increase your Mindful care-taking and set yourself a time-limit for a paperwork project and then stop, no matter what, so that you can pay attention to your other needs, such as family, food, and fun! (Again, don't you just love alliteration!)

WOW Factor!

It makes sense that if you make time for friends, family, fresh air, wholesome food, and lots of fun, you are far more likely to have energy and enthusiasm to meet the challenges of the working day. There must be balance in your day to sustain an inspirational teaching practice. A head teacher I recently trained explained that one of his greatest pressures was maintaining the "WOW" factor in school. There is no "WOW" if you are on your knees, exhausted, fed up, and overwhelmed. The "WOW" will be present when you are in balance, having had a fantastic break or relaxing weekend or simply an enjoyable evening out. When you are Mindful to put yourself first, ensuring plenty of 'oxygen' comes your way, you will have a spring in your step and be able to jump through all the hoops that arise, plus add in a song and a dance for a "WOW" moment along the way. Resentment is dissolved if you have assigned some quiet time for yourself, if you have been Mindful to assign time for self-care and nurturing. Stop and ask yourself how you approach a new day if you've had a great night out the night before. You've unconsciously told yourself that you have permission to relax and have fun as you've worked jolly hard that day. You return with a twinkle in your eye and a recharged, rebooted, and updated software package!

Your behaviour is likely to be more relaxed and tolerant to the scratchy elements of the day. Your buttons are less sensitive and less likely to react. If your stress buttons are triggered, you are more likely to manage them more healthily and bring them back to balance more easily and swiftly.

> *"Mindfulness-based interventions may be ideally suited to support the development of a mental set that is associated with effective classroom management... teachers reported significant reductions in emotional, behavioural, and gastronomic stress symptoms as measured by the Teacher Stress Inventory"*
>
> (TSI; Pettigrew & Wolf, 1982)

"Anyone can become angry — that is easy. But to be angry with the right person, to the right degree, at the right time, for the right purpose, in the right way - this is not easy."

The Nicomachean Ethics 383-322 BCE.

Benefits of Mindful Moments

The benefits of Mindful moments are far reaching. It is not just in your teaching life that shifts occur. Over time, with practise, you will exercise your acceptance muscle. Acceptance arises in the face of devastation and crisis. As your awareness grows, you begin to understand that the awareness that observes the drama stays constant. Even amongst unexpected tragedy, heightened emotion, or chaos, that which observes it all remains the same - peaceful and still. Imagine yourself as the eye of the storm; nothing is moving in the centre of it all. It is peaceful and still. The hurly-burly continues to whistle about you, and yet this awareness remains untouched. When you connect to this, there is freedom! Imagine how liberated you feel when this still point is in your awareness, especially when chaos abounds. The way you feel about your relationships, other peoples' behaviour, and how you approach your own inner critic, will change.

Mindful Awareness can initiate your heart opening. When your heart opens to your true self, your own beauty and magnificence, it will be ready to embrace others with compassion and understanding. Consider how the Dalai Lama responded when asked about self-hate. At first, he couldn't fathom the question. Eventually, he simply replied "What is that?" What if every teacher understood that a colleague or a child behaving inappropriately or unkindly is likely to be coming from a place of pain and/or confusion. With this understanding, they are more likely to respond Mindfully, Heartfully, and with compassion. Can you see how so many issues and situations that quickly escalate can be managed healthily and productively? In the long term, can you imagine how much time, energy, money and paperwork this would save!

The benefits of Mindful Moments for children are a thousand-fold. Children can be taught how to be "Still", how to access their Innocence, their silent awareness that is ever constant and peaceful. You can show them a new way to be and to learn in the classroom. You can give them techniques to access this internal awareness that will give them a sense of self, a sense of worth, and a resilience that will equip them not only for the challenges of learning, school-life and exams, but also for a deeper understanding of themselves, of others, and of how to make sense of all the different relationships they will experience in the world beyond school.

In time, hopefully, no matter how challenging they feel their life is, they can apply the principles outside the classroom too. All this obviously applies to you first. The more you practise and apply the techniques in the classroom and at home, the more you will have the Mindful muscles to support the young people to whom you have a duty of care. When you discover the shift in mental and emotional balance experienced through your Mindful practice, you will be drawn deeper into the inner world that brings this natural balance into awareness then into your reality.

The gift you bring your students when you introduce them to the infinite potential of their inner world is immeasurable. Just like you, they are aware of their inner machinations, but may not be consciously aware that they can take command of them. So often, they believe the negative inner critic and feel powerless to do anything about it. If they are overwhelmed by such unruly thoughts, berating themselves about how rubbish they are at maths or how useless they are at sport, they will soon buy into those noisy thoughts and believe them to be true. They will eventually identify themselves *as* those unhealthy thoughts and feel that they have no choice but to be (and act and behave) what they think and feel; the self-fulfilling prophecy.

You have the power to re-mind them of their power, to give them back their power. With Mindful moments, you can guide them back to balance. You can lift them out of their victim stories, their justifications, their aggression or confusion, and open their inner door to peaceful, supportive, healthy and balanced thoughts that will serve them to reach beyond their doubts and fears. As you become aware of *your* inner space, you can also generate opportunities for your students to explore theirs. Together, you will develop your emotional intelligence, raise your confidence or esteem, develop your patience, and feel calmer. When under pressure, you are more likely to manage the situation more healthily and behave appropriately, no matter what the challenge.

The key is that there is a deeper presence of mind that stimulates your natural state to be kind: kind to yourself, and kind to others. Can you see the value in this for you and your students? Can you imagine a world where kindness came first on the curriculum and children were taught how to understand and manage their emotions? So that when they felt frustration about not being able to calculate a sum, or not being able to write the words, they were praised and rewarded for recognising their heated feelings and for being present to it? Praised for understanding it is a natural response, and praised for managing it healthily, rather than being castigated for throwing the pencil and shouting angry words because they didn't know what to do with the frustrated volcano inside?

With your help and practice, you can be the one to show them by example that although feelings rise and fall, inside they can always return to that still realm of awareness, ever spacious and free, no matter what. You can bring them to a place of present-moment awareness and, with practice, guide them to be fully present throughout. You can help train their wandering minds, not through fear or chastisement, but through loving natural wisdom and deep connection with their own nature.

> *"Good teachers share one trait: they are truly present in the classroom, deeply engaged with their students and their subject... are able to weave a complex web of connections among themselves, their subjects and their students, so that their students can learn to weave a world for themselves. The connections made by good teachers are held not in their methods but in their hearts"*
>
> Parker Palmer, *The Courage to Teach.*

You can regularly ask the question "Am I *awake* now?" to yourself and to your children. Train your wandering mind! You can teach them how to develop and improve their concentration too. You will recognise that your concentration and ability to focus has improved and that this will benefit both you and your students. You will complete tasks more easily and therefore take less time on each task. You will become more efficient and effective at your job, improving your performance and that of your students, no matter what their ability, because you will *all* be present and in the right state to teach and learn. This will leave you more time to have fun in the classroom, plus friends-and-family time! Everyone's a winner!

I am not implying you can administer personality transplants at will. If children are determined *not* to listen, *not* to learn, and rather to disrupt, then Mindfulness may not be your first port of call. However, your response as a Mindful teacher is bound to be far more compassionate, patient and understanding than a mindless one!

The true magic of Mindful moments is that you are always at choice. You are never stuck if you are truly present. You need never live the lie of victim-thinking; you are always free.

> *"Mindfulness provides a simple but powerful route for getting ourselves unstuck, back in touch with our own wisdom and vitality."*
>
> Jon Kabat-Zinn

This diagram illustrates the simple path to bring you back to balance.

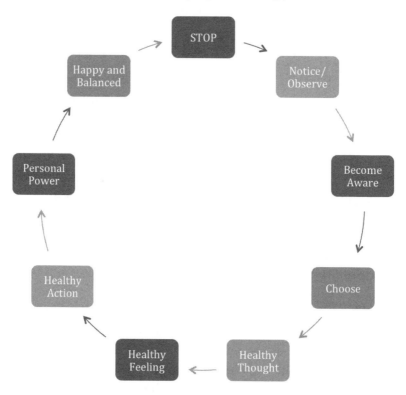

A study of secondary school teachers in the province of Granada, Spain analyzed the effects of a Mindfulness programme on teacher stress and the number of days of sick leave. The research confirmed that a *"significant reduction in the levels of teacher stress and the number of days sick leave was observed in the experimental group compared to the control group".*

> *"Nowadays, meditation techniques have sufficient scientific guarantee for the educational system to plan inclusion of these techniques into future teacher educational curricula, to prepare teachers with a series of tools and strategies which will enable them to effectively handle the situations of stress they face in their teaching practice."*
>
> Israel Manas, Clemente Franco Y Eduardo Justo 2011, University of Almeria, Spain.

Exploring Intention and Attention

"Intention is the conscious will to behave in a particular way and attention is the conscious focusing of awareness in order to perform the intention."

Dr.Shanida Nataraja *'The Blissful Brain'*.

You may ask yourself "What is my intention for this lesson?" This is very different from "what are my learning objectives and intended learning outcomes for this lesson". For a shift in effective teaching and for a nourishing teaching experience, I invite you always to look deeper when you set your intention for your lesson. When I am working one-to-one I will always ask my clients what their intentions are for their session. Some call it a prayer, some call it a wish, and some call it their highest intention. It doesn't matter to me what you call it. If you send your intention out with a pure heart, I believe it is more likely to be answered or met. This isn't some weird esoteric thing; it is simply setting your personal sat nav in a different way. If your focus is heart-centred and you have the highest intention for yourself and your students, you will be in flow. No matter that a child plays up or the fire alarm goes off, you will remain in your natural heart rhythm. Your intention will be met, even if not completely in a literal sense. If you speak from your heart and think heartful thoughts, you will act from the heart, even and especially when discipline is required.

> *"The thought manifests as the word*
> *The word becomes the deed*
> *The deed develops into the habit*
> *And the habit hardens into the character.*
> *So watch the thought and its ways with care,*
> *And let this spring from love*
> *Born out of concern for all beings."*

Words of wisdom attributed to the Buddha.

As a teacher I always tell my students that I am a learner too. In fact when I give a training session, I usually wear my "L" plate to highlight the fact that I am not setting myself up as a Master! I remind my learners that I am a learner of life and a learner of my craft, be it Drama, Art, Meditation, Mindfulness, or Parenting. I love to learn, and it is your privilege and honour to inspire the love of learning in the hearts and minds of these amazing young people who look up to you for guidance, care and inspiration.

Using Creative Visualisation is, as I've mentioned before, a fun and easy way to access your heart's desire and make it tangible. What is your vision of yourself as a successful, inspirational teacher? Contemplate and reflect on what you look like in this vision. In turn, you can inspire your students to do the same. If they have a vision, a picture or even a movie in their mind, they are more likely to feel and believe it as a possibility in their future reality (just like the gymnast). You will be able to paint a positive picture of what you want to be, of that extraordinary teacher who touches and opens the hearts of all she teaches. Similarly, you will have the internal resources to help each child paint a colourful, positive, and balanced picture of himself, not only as a learner of knowledge, but as a learner of life! What an amazing opportunity!

When teaching from the heart, it is important that you help make it meaningful for them. If you have a child who cannot see the value in what you are teaching, it is your responsibility to guide him to appreciate where the value may lay for him. You need to relate to his value system and link what you are teaching with his highest values. Dr. John Demartini is the master at teaching this! Only then will you capture his heart, and it will naturally begin to open to learning what you are teaching. I am not asking you to convince a child that your subject/lesson is important; I am inviting you to understand that if a child cannot see the point of the lesson, as it pertains to his life and his values, it will be much harder for him to listen and learn, never mind open his heart and mind to the magic of it!

I remember teaching a Year-9 boy drama. He hated drama, nor was it given a great deal of status in the school or in his timetable. (One single lesson fortnightly sent a clear message!) We were in a "sink" school (a school that is in a very poor area with few resources), smack in the middle of a massive council estate where learning wasn't perceived to be cool, and mucking about and bunking off were. The school was making massive strides to stem poor behaviour and shake off the horrendous reputation it had had for decades. Many of the teachers in the school were outstanding. However, the behaviour management was still mostly punitive, and the person who could shout or scream the loudest was often the most respected. I am not big on screeching to gain respect, not to say I didn't have to raise my voice on more than one occasion!

So there I was, up to my neck in rowdy Year-9 boys, some of whom were interested in drama, some of whom were happy to give it a go because it was a laugh, and some who just hated it. Those that hated it usually sat in two camps. They either did what they were asked begrudgingly for fear of detention or worse, or they didn't do anything and just didn't care what the consequences were.

This particular boy lacked confidence, and wasn't particularly sociable or academic. I'd got the majority of boys on task and was jollying along those that were slacking, when I was drawn to Mario, hovering against the wall trying not to be noticed so he didn't have to join a group. He was potentially volatile, as many of these beauties were. I asked him what was up. "What's the point? Drama's a waste of time".

In the past, I would have launched into why Drama was fantastic, fun and rewarding, but after listening to Dr John Demartini speak; I decided to ask him what he loved. What makes your heart sing? Actually I didn't use that language; he would have been out the door! "What *are* you interested in, Mario?" He said he had a mechanics placement, that he liked working on cars, and that he wanted to be a mechanic when he left school. Cool, now I could get digging. I asked him how drama might be useful to him as a mechanic. He looked at me blankly and with some prompting he started to get the idea. If you have customers, don't you need to know how to speak to them, provide good customer service, and build customer relations? I may have simplified the language. He saw how understanding body language would help him with his customers and perhaps work well with his colleagues and his boss. He began to see how his voice, his body language, and his ability to make eye contact may make or break a deal. You get the point.

We carried on exploring this until Mario could see the benefits of drama, even when the drama activity may be about Shakespeare! He joined a group and began to participate – awesome!

Now I know what you're thinking. That's all very nice, Kathryn, but I've got 30 kids in a room, I don't have time to do that for every single one of them every time I teach a new topic! I agree! What I am suggesting is that if you began a topic linking it to your students' highest values, being a kid their age and how it may benefit them, you may hook a few more in without any in-depth intervention. As a Mindful teacher, you may have the capacity to see past the belligerence and enquire as to what might really be stopping them from learning. Again, I concur, you cannot change their home environment or sub-culture, where learning may not be cool or respected, but you can wake them up to possibilities. If they stop and breathe and inquire why learning (not even subject-specific) might be useful to them, they may discover something quite unexpected. If you explored the notion that learning is beneficial to their ability to win the computer game, Mario Kart, they may just sit up in their seats and take notice. If you continue to explore this notion, your children are likely to come up with some fantastic reasons why it is helpful and worthwhile to learn, some of which you would never have thought of!

Remember you are working with exceptionally creative minds! Keep asking them every day why might it be useful to come to school? Why might it be helpful to learn about other countries and other cultures? Why might it be helpful to socialise, mix with other people, and be on time? And so on and so forth, until each child frequently asks himself the question on a regular basis and finds ways genuinely to link it to what they love. You will have sown a seed of magic for them for the rest of their lives to find balance in every situation – happy or sad, easy or difficult, kind or cruel. If you do the same for yourself, even the wretched paperwork will be a gift! Being present and aware to all of this, now this is true Mindfulness!

CHAPTER SEVEN

It Only Takes a Moment

It Only Takes a Moment

"Life is not measured by the number of breaths we take, but by the moments that take our breath away."

Anon

Threading Mindfulness Through Your Lesson

To some degree or another, you are already a Mindful teacher. I am simply reminding you of your magnificence and natural skills and providing new and easy ways to access your natural talents to implement them throughout your teaching day.

> *"Research indicates that contemplation and Mindfulness practices increase awareness of one's internal experience and promote reflection, self regulation, and caring for others."*
>
> (Ekman 2004)

Learning and teaching Mindfulness in school is not another "bolt-on" that someone on high has thought might be a good idea. You can personify Mindful qualities. You can live them! Being a Mindful teacher will bring about a new paradigm in teaching and learning. Mindful meditation leads to Mindful thought, Mindful actions, and Mindful experiences. You will already be Mindful of your children's needs and give them opportunities to support them. With Mindful techniques you are creating alternative ways to reach their hearts and minds. When Mindfulness is in your consciousness, you begin to choose Mindful ways to correct corruptive thinking, re-direct inappropriate behaviour, and address debilitating feelings and paralysing beliefs. You become the living example. You choose Mindful thoughts and actions. You teach, demonstrate, and lead Mindful thoughts and actions (rather than mind-less ones).

> *"Your chances of success in life are 80% determined by Emotional Intelligence and 20% by IQ."*

Will Ryan, Leadership with a Moral Purpose

There are so many practical applications, and I'm confident you will come up with many ways to apply the simple principles throughout your teaching day. Some will be more easily introduced at primary age than secondary. It will also depend on the type of school you are teaching in and the openness to new ideas and new approaches. Here are a few with which to experiment:

Assembly

When entering the hall, re-mind the children to walk slowly and with awareness of every step. If they are genuinely thinking about the way they are moving, they are less likely to enter as a noisy rabble! Re-mind them they are entering a place of community and togetherness (and if you are a Church school, you can of course add your ethos here.) Teach them how sacred and special this togetherness is. This is their opportunity to share and contribute just by being them, just by being part of something bigger than themselves - lots of little parts making a whole. The energy of the hall will feel different if they enter slowly and silently through Mindful choice, rather than because it is the rule. They may raise their consciousness and may even connect with the group consciousness and the message of the assembly. Through the Head's leadership, the children will practise being "Still". Learning to be in communion with the inner self whilst in a large group will be of enormous benefit to them. It will train their minds to be in "their business", to paraphrase Byron Katie, and to discipline their thinking. Practising together with their teachers will demonstrate the importance of this inner skill, which if practised regularly will improve their approach to learning, their ability to learn and, hopefully, their desire.

Entering Your Classroom

Invite your children to enter the room slowly and steadily. Spend a moment connecting with each child with a smile and eye contact. Do not let them enter until they have returned the eye contact. Even if they are not in the mood to smile, you will have shown them how valuable they are to you in that moment and be able to gauge how they are feeling. You may like to create a mood chart to reflect the mood they are in (again this is more suitable for primary). This brings them to awareness of how they are feeling, rather than being on grumpy Monday auto-pilot, and you can instantly take appropriate action if necessary. If you are teaching primary children, this repeated pattern can easily be incorporated into your routine. Invite them to sit at their desk and be still, even for one minute. Re-mind them to open their heart and be thankful for the opportunity to learn and be part of the class. They can thank their desk and Mindfully prepare for their first task. A gentle one-minute breathe-and-smile exercise would work a treat!

If you are teaching secondary children, you will find the time spent connecting and re-grouping their minds before they enter the room for your subject invaluable. You can set your expectations gently one-to-one, make them child-specific, and, if behaviour is not an issue, you can simply greet them with a smile and a warm welcome. The difference this will make and the impact this will create over time will be amazing. It will demonstrate how important everyone is. It will teach and prepare them for life. If they learn how powerful and personal a warm greeting can be, they are more likely to apply it when at an interview and when they are in charge of others as prefects or later in life as managers, for example. If they have had a challenging lesson prior to yours, a test, or results, they will bring those feelings, be they elation, irritation or indifference, into your classroom. You can nip in the bud any out-of-control behaviour and prevent any altercations that may be brewing, simply by setting your boundaries as they enter and re-minding them of your expectations.

This "check-in" time is also a great way to sort things out that may interrupt or prevent learning when in the classroom – needing the toilet, chewing gum, uniform discrepancies, antagonism, or brewing fights. Your Mindful manner will restore their balance and get them back in the right state for learning. Your balanced demeanour (no matter how chaotic the previous lesson) will demonstrate you have everything in order and in balance; that they are safe and welcome to learn in your special space.

Now I might not use that particular phrase in the classroom, but I would speak in the spirit of peace and love, especially when teaching in a school where violent behaviour, shouting, and fights were the norm. They took the micky sometimes, but they liked being in my class, even if they didn't like the subject matter, and they understood that a peaceful approach was expected. And, on the whole, this is what we all experienced, and they thrived. It was a starting point for genuine listening, sharing, and getting on task. It was also the bedrock for creativity to thrive, and as respect grew, there was more space for fun and laughter as we learnt together. No matter what the boys had experienced in the moments before entering my classroom, they were entering a new world, one which offered calmness and tranquillity.

An example of how powerful and helpful this can be, comes from when one of my students was being particularly belligerent in the corridor. My policy was not to allow them into my room until I had greeted them and done my "inner inventory" with them. This boy was known to be fiery, but had usually kept his cool in my class. Now, however, he was bouncing off the corridor walls, spitting fire. It was the norm to be shouted at and sent either to the head of department or even to the head teacher if such behaviour was being displayed, but instead of telling him to calm down, I simply asked him to wait for a moment whilst I settled the class. I then asked him to breathe, stand aside with me, and tell me what the matter was. His state shifted from anger to anguish in an instant. This tough kid choked up, tears began rushing down his face, and all his frustrations emptied. He was given the space he needed, an opportunity to pour out his despair. Once he had gathered his composure, he took another breath, entered my classroom calmly, by choice and at choice.

This scenario may have turned out very differently if I had not been Mindful that his behaviour was not who he really was. Keep your focus on the heart of the child, not the behaviour. When they learn that you are not there to judge them, but to guide them as best you can with the resources you have, there is a little more space for learning, sharing, caring, and changing unhealthy behaviour.

Please remember, I am not suggesting that being Mindful and applying Mindful techniques is a teacher's magic wand! It is a philosophy, an approach, and a set of techniques that can change the atmosphere of your classroom and your teaching over time and with practice. It is a wholesome way to manage challenges for yourself and your students. Sometimes it may not be what is required, and other actions may be necessary, but it is a fantastic place to start and a healthy way to create harmonious teaching and learning.

Register

You will have your own magical ways to bring your students to the present moment. You may gain their attention with clever clapping, arm signals, or even a music cue. Depending on your school environment, a particular stance or "look" may be all that is required! These are all Mindful techniques in so much as they bring your intention to their attention. You invite them to the present moment, where you then proceed to clarify desires and tasks in that moment. If behaviour isn't an issue and your children are able to concentrate well, you may not feel the need for additional Mindful cues. However, my experience is that you can prepare the child's mind-heart-body for learning with simple sensory stimulation. Perhaps put on the same piece of music as a one-minute warning that you will require silence at the end of the piece; burn incense or aromatherapy oils to create a welcoming, stimulating, or soothing atmosphere for the beginning of your teaching day; or invite a child gently to ring a tingsha bell as a signal for calm, sitting still, and listening time.

Using the senses as a regular cue to come to calm and quiet is a simple and easy way to prepare for teaching and learning. It works in a similar way to Pavlov's reflex. The mind-heart-body responds to the cue, and the muscle memory remembers what will happen and triggers the appropriate hormones to influence the physical, mental, and emotional action. These essential strategies, known as anchors, are simple and effective.

Play Time

I am an advocate of lots of free play, no matter what age the children. Kids are great at knowing what to do and how to play to fulfil their individual needs. My only invitation is regarding safety and the use of "clean" language to ensure this. For example, if you see a child sprinting down a corridor, you remind the child to "Walk!", rather than calling out "Don't run!" This is because the brain will not hear the negative, and negative commands can *encourage* disobedience. By the same token, "Jamie, please whisper!" is a more useful instruction than "Jamie, don't shout!"

You may already know this; however it's great to be re-minded. It changed my parenting and my teaching when I discovered this simple application. Hence "Hold your drink carefully!" rather than "Don't spill your drink!" You get the idea. Your desired end-result is clear and precise, and this approach makes a huge difference to speaking and listening. Especially when it's loud-and-lively time, like break or lunch times, this linguistic nuance can cut down drastically on energy and accidents. If you want to learn more about this, listen to my *Verbal Aikido For Teachers* audio programme, created in association with Dr. Topher Morrison, master practitioner and trainer of Neuro-linguistic Programming (NLP). This will give you some extraordinary insights and techniques to communicate effectively.

Wet Play

Again, you will have lots of fabulous strategies already for happy and safe 'wet play', but you may be exasperated by the post-wet-play energy and resultant behaviour. Bring the children's awareness to their bodies. Invite them to have a contained stretch, wiggle, or maybe a dance for a few minutes. Get them really into their bodies and focus their energies so that it can be channelled and released happily and appropriately. You may invite them to do a body scan, squeezing all their muscles and then slowly watching their muscles uncurl and release. Even a quick 'shake it out' and breathing exercise will help them release all that unexpressed energy and relax for the lesson. You can apply all of the above to fidgets too! Complete the experience by bringing them to quiet and calmness through their Power Breath. Invite the children to focus on their end-result in all Innocence. Invite them to see themselves happy, having completed the task.

The Power Breath

"Breath is the bridge which connects life to consciousness, which unites your body to your thoughts. Whenever your mind becomes scattered, use your breath as the means to take hold of your mind again."

Thich Nhat Hahn

Throughout this book, I have referred to the breath as a key component to bring yourself into balance. You will know that when a child is upset, hysterical even, the first thing you instinctively get them to do is to take some deep breaths. This way, you can understand what they are saying and they can regulate themselves. The breath is a truly magical mechanism. It is one of the very few bodily functions that occurs unconsciously and that we can control consciously. It affects all 11 systems in the body - cardiovascular, digestive, respiratory, skeletal, urinary, reproductive, endocrine, lymphatic, integumentary (skin), muscular, and nervous systems.

The breath influences the way we are and act on a mental, physical and emotional level. The breath is the gateway to the present moment. It is the easiest, simplest, and most effective way to bring yourself back from wherever you were, past or future, and direct your attention to NOW! Your breath is the key to Mindful awareness. It is the natural way to manage stressful thoughts and the feelings that ensue. The breath brings your attention inside your body and to this moment. This moment is ultimately all you have. In "this" moment, there is Peace. There is nothing but peace. If you bring all your attention to "this" moment and are truly present to "this" and nothing else, you are in a state of now, where nothing exists except "thisness". You are free in "this moment", and there is no suffering, no longing for things to be different, and no yearning for things that could be. Just this. Just now. And when your awareness is fully present to "this", you are all powerful.

This is why I named this particular breathing technique The Power Breath. You bring yourself to a powerful place when you are truly present. When you are poised and present, you are in charge of the way you respond to "what is". You are in full awareness of yourself "at choice". There is liberation and freedom. There is no right or wrong. There is no judgement. When you bring yourself to "this", there is peace.

The Power Breath is simple. You gently move your attention to your tummy with the intention of breathing from a deeper place. Our tendency when stressed or anxious is to breathe from the upper thorax, high up in the chest. Your breath is usually faster and shallower. If you are in a real pickle, you may feel like you are breathing in your throat, that you are holding your breath, or even unable to breathe at all! So bring your breath from the upper chest down into your abdomen. If you have ever done yoga, acting, or singing classes, you may be familiar with this. It is easiest to learn this technique lying down, just so you can totally relax your body and keep your attention on your breath. Lie down in a centred position and allow your body to relax and feel supported by the floor or bed. Place one hand on your chest and one on your tummy. A word for all you ladies: our society is always telling us girls to hold our tummies in. Just for once, I invite you to let go of your belly. No-one is watching, and your eyes will be closed so you won't be able to see either!

Simply watch your breath as it naturally goes in and out. Notice which hand rises. Is your breath in the chest or in your tummy? There is no right or wrong, just observe. There are benefits and drawbacks to different types of breathing in different situations. It is helpful to notice where your breath is located when you are at rest, but not to worry where it is at the beginning. It is where it is, and that is fine. For the purposes of deep relaxation in this instance, you will be guiding your breath down to your tummy. When you adopt the Power Breath, it may at first feel counterintuitive; however, it is your natural breath state. If you watch a new born baby, you will notice that his little tummy is rising and falling naturally as he breathes.

Begin by taking a nice deep breath in. Imagine you have a balloon inside your tummy, and as you breathe in, the balloon is getting bigger, and as you breathe out, your balloon deflates. If you find this tricky at first, relax and just play around with making your tummy look like Mr Greedy from the Mr Men. When your tummy muscles and your brain get the hang of what it feels like and know what is meant to happen, you will relax. Repeat. Fill your tummy with fresh new oxygen as you breathe in, and as you breathe out, release the stale air. Obviously, you are not literally filling your tummy with air; you may want to clarify this when you teach your students - your lungs are not in your stomach - but it feels like it! What you are doing is filling the lower lungs more efficiently by moving your diaphragm out of the way, so that your lower lungs can fill and expel more easily. When your lungs are working at optimum level, you will increase the levels of oxygen in your blood and, therefore, your brain and muscles. You don't need me to tell you what the advantages of this will be for effective teaching and learning!

Bring both your hands down to your tummy, close your eyes, and practise your Power Breath. If you get it straight away, great. If you find it awkward and difficult, that's great too. It's just an invitation to practise and to give yourself the gift of a new way of breathing. Don't get hung up on it, just relax and practise until it feels natural. Once you feel comfortable with the belly breathing, you can invite the mind to join in and do a job too. This helps the mind relax and make sense of the relaxation experience, and it prevents the 'monkey-mind' chatter from taking over and defeating the whole point of the exercise.

For deep relaxation, you want to have a **longer exhale**. Start with a count of three as you breathe in and a count of five when you breathe out. If this feels easy, exhale for seven. There is no right or wrong way to do this. Experiment. You may find a breath in of five is right for your lung capacity, or you may feel more comfortable with a smaller breath to start with. Just as you are fingerprint-unique, so too is your breathing pattern. What you find comfortable, your colleague may not. Go at your own pace and listen to your natural body rhythm. Work within that and enjoy the relaxation sensations that it brings.

The Power Breath will bring you to the present moment. It will bring you to 'now' easily and effortlessly. It is your body's natural life saver. It will keep you calm and enable you to manage your reactions more healthily. It can prevent a knee-jerk response and give you a moment to gather your thoughts and compose your feelings before you respond. You will then be in charge of yourself. You can respond healthily and prevent a volcanic outburst. You can guide yourself naturally to a state where you are in charge. When you are stressed and angry, you can easily give your power away. By using the Power Breath, you stay in charge, you make decisions that will serve you and support your emotional health and well-being.

No doubt you will recognise just how valuable this technique can be in the world of teaching. Whether you are in a challenging staff meeting or with a challenging group of students, you can stay in charge of your thoughts, feelings and actions. I remember in my first year of teaching being with a Year-9 class. My Nan was dying, and I was not fully present with this class which had a few very challenging girls in it. I was teaching in a room not built for purpose, and it was far too big. Managing the space was hard enough, and managing the behaviour was even trickier, especially as a newbie! Picture the scene if you will. Gina was being her usual lairy self and was not in the mood for learning. She was not big on conforming at the best of times, and she had vast amounts of unexpressed anger. The short version is that she consistently ignored my requests and continued to ignore my direction. She was eager to challenge authority, and I was not asserting it effectively.

After many attempts at redirection and encouraging her to get on task, I became exasperated. I made the classic mistake of entering into an unhealthy exchange which soon escalated. She goaded me with all sorts of delightful taunts, and then I snapped. I got angry, I raised my voice, lost control of myself, and burst out with "my Nan's dying and all you can do is....." You can fill in the gaps! As soon as I raised my voice I knew I'd blown it. If I recall correctly, she announced how she didn't give a monkey's that my Nan was dying and then stormed out of the classroom. I could do nothing to stop her as she exited from the other end of this vast corridor of a room (which had once been sleeping dorms in the 1800s!!!) I was left humiliated and without an ounce of teaching self-worth. When I closed the lesson and returned to my mentor with my tail firmly between my legs, I felt ashamed and hopeless about the way I had handled, or rather not handled, the situation.

My strong, assertive, head of faculty was awesome. I was afraid she would berate me, but as I was clearly doing such a good job of that independently, she counteracted my thoughts. She gave me advice, support and encouragement to do it differently next time. It was the end of a half term and she suggested I could reassert myself at the beginning of the new half term and set my boundaries and codes of conduct again. Not only did she implicitly give me permission to make mistakes, she reassured me it was simply a learning curve I needed to experience and master. The truth is that even without the behaviour management skills, I would have managed myself so much better if I had stayed in charge of myself and not let my oversensitivity get the better of me. I was in a raw emotional state and not in the right frame of mind for effective teaching, never mind inspiring learning. I thought I could cope as I was great at wearing masks – I was a trained actor for heaven's sake! But when the chips were down, I did not have enough *resources* to cope. If only I had known how to take charge of myself through my breathing. I would definitely have done it differently and dealt with the pressure of a very demanding and unpleasantly behaved young woman along with the emotional distress of not being with my Nan as she was leaving this world.

The first step is to catch your breath. Stay in awareness of how you are feeling and what is happening to your state. Over time, you will begin to recognise when you are losing your equilibrium and getting out of balance. Catch your breath and bring your attention to your breathing if there is something brewing in you or your classroom. Step two is to befriend your breath. Make friends with the number-one tool that is the bringer of balance and your natural defence against stress. When you are good friends with someone, you spend quality time with them, you pay attention to them, and you visit often. This is your job with your breath. It may sound a little crazy, but if you honour your breath consciously, as you would a new best friend, you can lean on your friend in a crisis.

There is a deep connection and a level of trust that will enable you to rely on your breath when you need it. You will be so in tune with it that it will come naturally to you, empowering you to stop and be "Still". You will instinctively focus on your breathing as you notice a swell of frustration or anger arising within you that may be unhelpful to express. You will use your breath to stay in charge of yourself, your thoughts, feelings and subsequent actions.

Please note I avoid using the term "in control". If you are in control, it implies there is a forcing, a striving, or a pushing to keep control. I prefer staying "in charge". This suggests I have a negative and positive charge and I choose to stay in balance of these two polarities. Control is restrictive, constricting, and holding. *In charge* is balanced, wholesome, healthy, and assertive, without the need to grip tightly.

There are lots of breathing exercises you can embrace and all sorts of techniques you can learn. Explore the teachings of pranayamic breathing in yoga and Jill R Johnson's 'Oxycise' for two great breathing technique options. Optimal breathing is breathing in for a count of seven, holding for seven, and breathing out for seven. You can explore and embrace the various techniques available to you. I advocate *The Power Breath* because it is simple, immediate, and easy to apply in everyday situations. The invitation is to embrace your breath and to understand it can empower you throughout your teaching day and throughout your life. It is a natural gift! You may take it for granted, but when you embrace it, make friends with it and employ this natural resource in your everyday life and in the classroom, you will undoubtedly reap the benefits!

Even the simplest of breath moments can have a positive impact on your day. Before the family tuck in to dinner, I request just a moment's pause to breathe. We "Namaste" (honour each other's diamond), and this gives us a moment to connect with the blessings of our food, our family, and this moment of togetherness. It's all there in a breath. It takes only a breath. Simplicity, calm, and power all lie present in your breath. These qualities and more are simply a thought away, a breath away. Why wouldn't you use them?

If you are nervous at the beginning of your lesson for whatever reason (maybe Ofsted inspectors are lurking, maybe you are testing out new material, maybe it's your first day in a new school), you can employ the Power Breath to re-centre yourself and come back into balance. The breath will take you out of your mind (where all the incessant mind chatter is unsettling you) and bring you back into your body. When you are present in your body, you cannot entertain the negative and destructive thoughts that betray your equilibrium. It only takes a moment to draw in the powerful influence of your breath, and the beauty of it is that no-one knows you're doing it. You don't need to look like the wolf in the Three Little Pigs. There is no need to huff and puff. Just quietly and gently draw in peace and tranquillity that is always available to you with a few slow, deep breaths. Use your imagination to support your breath, and imagine breathing in calm, and breathing out stress, if that helps you.

It may sound too simple. What's the catch? There isn't one. Your challenge is to trust your breath and to be aware of the resistance that may arise to employing your most natural resource. I was recently asked by a fellow teacher what she should do to manage her infestation of fury. She was feeling wound up and fed up by a series of situations that were fast escalating (partly thanks to a looming inspection that had sent the entire education senior management into a paperwork frenzy!) I taught her the Power Breath with a twist, adding the smiling meditation. She did three deep Power Breaths with me, and on the out breath she smiled. She said after the experience she was still wound up! It hadn't got rid of the feelings.

Aha, said I. You simply need to keep repeating the technique until something shifts. She stopped, refocused, and returned to her breath. It calmed her down, and later in the day, she recognised how much it had helped her.

The Power Breath cannot CHANGE your thoughts; it can simply bring your attention to your body and invite you to release those damaging thoughts which will be generating the unpleasant feelings. It is interesting that sometimes, actually let's be honest oftentimes, you may want to hold onto those outraged thoughts because you are "in the right" and your ego-mind wants to keep you safe and keep you self-righteous. But the need to be right and to express how right you are, only serves to feed those thoughts and feelings that keep you stuck in the vicious and unpleasant cycle of negativity and heightened emotion. I know, I've done it often and still to this day catch myself doing it, especially when it comes to family behaviours that push my buttons. I haven't got it sussed, but I am aware of the buttons I have yet to unplug!

> *"It helps to have a focus for your attention, an anchor line to tether you to the present moment and to guide you back when the mind wanders. The breath serves this purpose exceedingly well".*
>
> Jon Kabat-Zinn

The breath is a beautiful mechanism to bring you into awareness; then you can choose what state you really want to be in. It brings you to the present moment and brings you to choice. It creates the most loving opportunity to open your heart. When you embrace your Power Breath, you can instantly melt the armour around your heart and mind and choose another thought. You can choose a healthy thought. If you want to stay "right", do what you've always done and follow the thoughts that insist and "prove" you are right. If you want to feel balanced, embrace your breath and let your most powerful natural resource support healthy choice in the face of challenge and change. I have a lovely meditation card that reminds me "I can always reach for a thought that feels better".

You can support your mind-heart-body with different patterns of breathing for different situations and differently desired outcomes.

To relax:

Choose a longer exhale. For example, breathe in for three, breathe out for seven. This is great to help you relax after a demanding day in the classroom and to release the tension before bed. It will help you relax, let go, and ease you into sleep.

To energise:

Choose a longer inhale. For example, breathe in for seven and out for three! This will help you reconnect with your natural energy source in your body and invigorate your cells. It will help sharpen the mind if you are experiencing the three o'clock lull and you need to be clear and present for a parent's evening or a staff meeting, where nodding off may not be appreciated!

To balance:

Choose a rhythm of equal in and out breaths. Breathe in for seven, hold for seven, and breathe out for seven, or whatever number works for you as you develop these skills. (Just so long as it's the same number for each) This will help you bring yourself fully into balance. You will recalibrate your entire mind-heart-body. You will bring your thoughts, muscles, and oxygen flow into balance, creating homeostasis -"the ability or tendency of an organism or cell to maintain internal equilibrium by adjusting its physiological processes". thefreedictionary.com.

Ultimately, bringing your attention to your breath, feeling the breath, experiencing the breath flowing gently in and gently out, provides all the resources you need to be fully present in the moment. Witnessing and experiencing the wonder of the breath without having to fix, change, or control it, is where your true power and inspiration lie. It only takes a moment to return your attention to your breath, and you only need be fully present for one full-in breath and one full-out breath. If you keep your attention fully with this one cycle of breath, you will be in the now and ready and able to manage the moment that follows. You do not need to make an effort, to push, strive or exert your will over your breath, to be fully present to it. Simply ask if you are awake to that breath and softly observe it. It is the most natural and organic mechanism in your body. Invite and allow it to support and guide you in each moment.

Find a comfortable position. Feel supported by the chair (or floor or bed). Take a slow deep breath in, and as you breathe out, bring your awareness to your breathing. Notice the cool air enter through your nose, and as you breathe out, notice the warmth of the air gently stroking your skin. Bring all your attention to your breath, filling up your tummy with fresh oxygen. Then release all the stale air and negative thoughts as you breathe out. Feel your mind and body flowing effortlessly in harmony as your breath flows gently in and gently out. Observe your breathing and the natural mechanism of in-breath and out-breath. Stay focussed on the natural rhythm without forcing or changing it. Stay present to your breath and enjoy its power to calm your mind and strengthen your heart.

CHAPTER EIGHT

You Can't Stop the Waves...

You Can't Stop the Waves...

"You can't stop the waves, but you can learn to surf."

Jon Kabat-Zinn

It Only Takes a Moment

You will appreciate that through gentle awareness of each moment, your entire teaching experience can become a Mindful practice. By staying present and welcoming the present moment as it is and noticing what arises, you will be embracing the implicit messages within Mindfulness. You will be compassionate towards what is. Your compassion will swell not only for your students but hopefully also for yourself. You will be less likely to judge harshly and more likely to embrace an attitude of non-judgement. Harshness will be replaced with kindness. I am not suggesting you are not a kind teacher already, but sometimes the pressures of testing, curriculum fulfilment, meeting deadlines, and overcoming borderline abilities to improve scores, can overwhelm you, colour your thinking process, and how you act and react to situations. Mindfulness simply helps you stay awake to your natural Heartfulness.

It is when teaching comes from the heart that openings occur. The learning environment blossoms, and the boundless nature of creativity and possibilities broaden. Natural wisdom and human potential, for both you and your students, ignite, especially for children who are despondent or uninterested due to fear of failure, or who are challenged by learning difficulties such as dyslexia. Labels can be helpful or harmful, but a Mindful teacher can look beyond the label and connect with the child. She can also guide the child to let go of the label that they identify with and find a new understanding of themselves that helps, rather than hinders, them.

Awareness brings about an understanding, or at least the beginnings of a glimpse of an understanding, of the "bigger picture". It invites you to connect with something that is ever present. It is this "constant" that oversees our play dough life of activity and dramas! When you plug into this you are more able to keep things in perspective, bring yourself back to balance, and feel calm in the chaos. This awareness invites trust, strength, and inner resources. You begin to trust your heart, and you focus on how your heart wants the lesson to go. You see beyond behaviour and look deeper for the root cause of the behaviour. Your line of enquiry, when clashes and chaos arise, is compassionate. This does not mean you are not strict and clear with boundary setting; simply you apply appropriate discipline with clarity and kindness. There is an underlying acceptance of what shows up. The ego-mind wants to control everything, but a Mindful teacher will be present with what is and accept the flow of learning, behaviour, and interruptions, whilst being fully present to address what occurs.

This does not mean you are passive to classroom rioting! It simply means you create an environment that has clear, loving parameters and the ability to go with the ebb and flow of the reality in the classroom. There is no point getting cross and frustrated that Jamie has a guitar lesson half way through your fantastic revelation of the solar system! There is no point fighting against reality when Tidjani has a dental appointment and his departure disrupts your concentration and the focus of your class, or when the fire alarm goes off because Davey is clowning around again and crucifies an important exam practise. Getting agitated and wound up will only serve to dismantle your ability to teach effectively and will inevitably affect learning. By all means, be absolutely present with your feelings - I am not suggesting you suppress them - but simply observe them for what they are, stay still in the moment of heightened emotion, without getting attached to them. Feel the annoyance, watch how it makes you respond physically, watch the unhelpful thoughts cloud your mind, and then release them. Or at least turn the volume right down on them! Return to the present moment and you will be free to assign your attention to your initial intention for your lesson.

> *"Let gentleness my strong enforcement be."*
>
> William Shakespeare

In these ways, you will not only be able to deal with your worry; you will be able to support your children with *their* worries, spoken or unspoken. You will be aware and open to understand and address the issues compassionately. With Mindful awareness, when you help children who are upset, you will be strong in your gentleness and are less likely to take on board their pain. You will meet their pain and guide them to their own internal resources that will re-mind them of their inner strength and their diamond qualities. You will orientate them to calmness and equilibrium. Ultimately, you will inspire them to self-empower, to explore solutions for themselves.

This is the best teaching gift you can give a child. Yes, you can break up fights, but what if you could invite them to see the other boy's perspective? What if you could create an opening for personal awareness that would reduce the chances of them fighting in the first place? It sounds idealistic and impossible perhaps, but what if you could open the door to a new way, to a world of different possibilities that they may have never thought of before, all because you have become Mindfully aware of what is?!

Battling with what is, is like fighting quicksand. I vividly remember watching an old Tarzan film when I was a child. I watched a man fall into quicksand and fight for his life. He panicked and struggled, and I would scream at the telly "Don't move! Don't struggle! Stop! Wait! Help is coming! Stay still!!!" How interesting if you applied this to yourself and your students when stressful thoughts and painful feelings are sucking you under! The less you struggle or battle with what is, the easier it is to be pulled out of the negative and destructive cycle. The harder you fight reality and struggle with what is, the deeper you go. You get stuck, or worse, you get overwhelmed, swamped, and drown. A simple application of Mindful breathing can give you enough time, space and awareness to approach the problem differently; you can take healthy action to overcome, work with or steer around the perceived problem.

"You can't stop the waves, but you can learn how to surf" is one of my favourite quotes from Jon Kabat-Zinn. It is the best metaphor I know for capturing the imagination of anyone I work with. The child who feels like nothing is fair, and that he cannot control the way he feels or behaves, can ride the waves of his imagination. So too can the trainee teacher who spends hours on lesson planning, only for the observed lesson to go belly up, the conscientious teacher who rarely receives a thank you, or the exhausted head who receives abuse from a parent, and so on.

Jump on your board and surf with me for the ride of your teaching life! What I imagine makes surfing such a thrill is that you have absolutely no control over the waves! This makes the experience both scary and exciting! You are not in charge of how big the waves are and you have zero control of how thick and fast they will come. The only thing you can be in charge of is how you *respond* to the waves. You are there out on the open ocean, nothing but you, your board, and your wits. Your mind-heart-body is alert to each moment. You identify the shifts in the swell, when there is a slight change in the wind and the movement of the currents. It is you embracing nature. You do not fight what is there. You simply brace yourself, focus, and do your best to not only stay on but to ride the wave. The beauty of surfing is that you have the gift of being connected to your board! So if a tsunami-like wave does knock you off your board, maybe because you were not paying attention or because you just couldn't have predicted its enormity, you do not need to search for your board. It is always with you. You have a safety line. When the wave crashes, you can cling on to your board and wait. Even if the water has rushed up your nose and is stinging your eyes and has knocked the wind out of you, you can simply hang on in each moment and stay still. If you begin thrashing about for your surfboard, you will only push it out of reach. Just stop! Wait a moment and the board will be there and come to you. When you have caught your breath, literally and metaphorically, you can once again climb aboard. If you feel exhausted and maybe even despairing that you'll never get the hang of surfing (or teaching), you can simply clamber atop your board and stay there. The ocean will support you, and you can simply bob along for a while, lying flat, not trying to move, change, or steer anything. The board will keep you afloat, and the ocean will ensure you gently move in the direction that is natural for that moment. You work with the tide, not against it.

And so after a while you choose to stand back up on your board. You may have jelly legs and you may not feel very sure of yourself, but you manage to regain your equilibrium once more. Maybe someone has helped you up; maybe you remembered what your instructor taught you. You bring your attention to the task in hand and make a decision to start surfing again. You focus on your destination; you set your personal sat nav. You may paddle about for a while first, deciding on the best location and the most appropriate direction; you will assess the conditions of the sea and the weather; and eventually you step back up to the challenge.

The surfing may be a little wobbly and awkward at first. You may feel nervous and lack the confidence you had before you were knocked off, but over time and with a lot of practice you will learn to ride the waves! You will be surfing with the highs and the lows. You will learn how to manoeuvre those tricky currents and you will have your wits about you to predict the adjustments you need to make to stay afloat. You will be equipped with the internal resources to manage the changes and challenges that the surf brings. Your awareness brings you greater understanding of the ocean and how to flow *with* the current, not against it. Nothing has changed. The one constant you can rely on is that everything is moving, shifting, and changing in every moment, and you are breathing! The only thing that remains calm, still, and peaceful is the awareness of it all. And one day you will notice that you are riding the waves in style. You are riding, carving, and gliding through the water not as a separate entity on top of the ocean but as part of the ocean, no separation, just one with the board, the waves, and nature.

I don't need to spell out the correlation between surfing and teaching. It's all there for you to enjoy exploring at your leisure!!! I will however bring to your attention a few issues that may be useful to address.

Things Out of Your Control

You cannot change a child's circumstances; you can only address their experiences in your arena. In school, you can provide them with a safe and nurturing environment. You can teach them your expectations, the norms and values of the school and of your classroom. I remember my dear friend Jayne returning home after her first teaching practice in our first year at Uni. She was teaching in a very deprived area with high rates of child protection and issues of neglect. She was upset that she had to leave them each day, knowing that they were going back to challenges she didn't want to imagine. She wanted to bring them home with her and make it all better for them. It was difficult to comfort her when facing her first tsunami.

I too recall teaching some terrific Year-10 boys, many of whom had been labelled BESD and ADHD (Attention Deficit Hyperactive Disorder) and were very low achievers. There was one boy in particular, Dan, who was somewhat challenging to teach. He (and his uniform) needed a nice hot bath and time to soak in the bubbles. He was very volatile and had a very difficult home life. But I always admired him for coming in to school. No-one outside school would have noticed or castigated him if he hadn't gone to school, but he chose to get himself up every day, put on his uniform, and show up. He wasn't very good at drawing, but discovered he was a natural with clay. He made a beautiful tile piece and actually allowed me to take a photo of him with his work. But the next time I saw him, he had destroyed all his work. He was caught in the vicious cycle of deprivation and self-loathing. He was tired, confused, and angry. He didn't have the resources to surf in a different direction, but he still climbed back on his board every day.

Both Jayne and I wanted to rescue these beautiful young people. We felt they deserved better, deserved more, and deserved a chance. But my years of paddling about on the ocean have taught me that it is not my responsibility to change their reality. It *is* my responsibility to provide a healthy environment in the classroom, so that they can choose how to cope and how to manage the ups and downs. I am not so arrogant as to think I know what someone's surfing (healing) path is. I cannot see and do not know their bigger picture. What may seem like unnecessary suffering in this moment may be laying the foundations for liberation, enlightenment, and inspiration in the future. You (and I) can simply offer them the magical moments in the classroom during the time that you have with them. You can offer them your passion, compassion and wisdom. You can offer them opportunities to learn and be inspired by learning, so that they can then choose where they want to go and what they want to be and do. You can bring them to awareness that their difficulties, challenges or obstacles may be fantastic opportunities to grow, learn, and change. You can show them that they do not have to be a victim to their thoughts, feelings, or circumstances; that they can make a choice in every moment as to how they respond to the outside by being strong and still on the inside. You can invite them to enquire what the gift might be in their perceived suffering.

My brother Richard has severe dyslexia. When he was growing up, there was no such thing as dyslexia; it wasn't recognised the way it is today. He was labelled lazy and stupid. He retreated into his bedroom and stayed there. In his adult years, he admitted to having been bullied incessantly for his entire senior school life. Even though he was built like a brick house, he was not one to fight. He chose to turn the other cheek and walk away. If only he had been given the resources that we have now, not only the practical support that could help him read, write and communicate, but also the emotional tools to rebalance his perceptions about his "disability". However, looking back (hindsight is so handy!), he and I can both see that the unpleasant experiences he went through served to build his personal resilience. He became a very determined young man and made a decision that he would make his fortune and retire at 40. Just before his 40th birthday, he sold his business in the United States and fulfilled his promise to himself.

Does that sound like a person who is lazy and stupid to you? When I work with children that have very low self-esteem, feel like they'll never amount to anything, that they are already bottom of the heap, I always tell them about my amazing brother who not only made something of himself but also helped many troubled children and young people in the process. He is an inspiration and a living example of how to cling on to your surfboard till you've mastered how to stand up on it, then to persist until you can keep your balance, no matter what the weather. Eventually, you will be flying through the rips and living your purpose through contribution and creativity!

It can feel hard not to take on responsibility for children that have it tough, but through Mindful enquiry, you will see how important it is to let go of feeling responsible for the life of your children. Yes, you are responsible for teaching and inspiring them to learn, but you are not responsible for wrapping them up in cotton wool and putting plasters on their emotional wounds. You have the privilege and opportunity to be present with them – fully present - in each moment you are together. You can give them what you believe they require in that moment, but only in that moment. You can let go of the need to make it *right* for them and to make everything better for them as you perceive it. In their eyes, they may already feel everything is just fine or they may feel more than capable to manage their situation themselves. It is your gift to guide them to the choices available to them. By bringing them into awareness of their choices and their personal inner power, you will be giving them the gift of self-empowerment and self-respect. They can then choose if they want more help. If they are offered help, they will know if they want to have it or at least have the skills to express their confusion or indecision. You can lead by example. You can give them someone to aspire to and someone to admire, as they learn to discern who and what they want to be.

You can PRAISE your students as much as you can. Authentic praise fills the recipient, and the giver, with joy and pride. The power of genuine praise can never be underestimated. Reassure, reassure, reassure! No matter where you or a child is on his learning surfing path, it is always constructive and pleasant to give and receive praise, encouragement, and reassurance.

The System

You can't necessarily change the system; you can only change your response to it. After six months of working in a juvenile unit for young women offenders, I was so incensed by the archaic system and the lack of care for the emotional needs of these young women, some of whom were serving life, that I quit. (There were other factors of course, but this was a huge issue!) I was repeatedly reminded by the head of education that it was not my job to improve their emotional health or address their attitude (which was often disturbing, alarming, and unbalanced). I was there to teach them a subject and that was it! Aaagggh!

Those young women were clearly out of balance, in a lot of pain, and often very confused. I wanted to scream at the system, give it a good shake, and tell them what healthy action would be glaringly obvious to take. For example, there were 16 women in the unit. A counsellor visited once a week and had four time slots. You do the math! What about the other twelve women? However, it did not serve me or the young women to rage at the system. The prison system is the prison system is the prison system. Right there, right then, there was nothing I could do to change it in the role I was in at that time. I chose not to battle with the system. In retrospect, had I really wanted to do something about it, I could have; I just didn't have the resources, the knowledge and the understanding of the system to make that decision at the time.

Similarly, you are working in a system that in many respects is also antiquated. The definition of Education is "a process of teaching, training and learning, especially in schools or colleges, to improve knowledge and develop skills" (Oxford Advanced Learners Dictionary). The education system was formalised in England and Wales with the introduction of the Elementary Education Act in 1870. The Act created the framework for a basic curriculum for children aged 5 to 12 years, largely to keep Britain competitive in the newly industrialised world. In the 21st century, with all the modern technology and sophisticated systems in our society, we are still on the whole teaching by rote. This worked very well for the Victorians but, in the 140-odd years since, may have outlived its usefulness as a means to furnish young people with the skills they require to survive and thrive in a very different world.

My eldest son is just completing his first year at secondary school. He is a bright young man who loves to learn. He was born with a very hungry and curious mind. He worked hard to gain a place at the local grammar school, for which competition is fierce as children come in from miles around. But he spent his first year feeling deeply disappointed, disillusioned, and frustrated. The system is so inflexible by Year 7 and doesn't serve his creative mind. He finds many of the subjects irrelevant and lack meaning to his life.

His disillusionment is far from unique. Go to the other end of the spectrum, where children have not been encouraged to study nor inspired by academics, and there too is a big crater of a gap in the system. The system is not meeting the needs of the learners – not for all, but for many. The conformists work well and are praised in a system that focuses on conformity and sometimes passive learning. More and more, children are spoon-fed the way to answer questions to ensure they give the "right" answer. This ensures that targets are met, that C/D borderline kids don't bring down the statistics, and that the league tables rule.

This is not an indictment of teachers; it's a reflection on a system that focuses on one main measurement of success – exams. Who cares if the kids don't have any communication skills or personal resilience or the resources to handle rejection; who cares if they do not understand how their body language, tone of voice, or facial expressions can make or break an interview or first impression; who cares if they do not understand the importance of meaningful relationships or how to manage themselves in sexual situations; who cares if they can't cook an egg, make dinner, or know the difference between healthy and unhealthy food choices?

You may say that all these issues are covered in various subjects now. That may in part be true, but how much theory is applied in practice? Young people do not need 15 GCSEs to move onto 'A'-levels. Why not study six or seven and leave space to play, explore their passions, exercise, socialise, and develop personal skills to manage life situations? Why should all these be an add on? Give them time to BREATHE! Give them space to BE!

One motto I have is "Stop Whining and start Winning!" By all means take a moment to have a rant at the system too, but understand that unless you are prepared to take action about your bugbears, let it go! It serves no-one to fight the system internally. It will just make you ill. I know! I generated so much internal stress in my mind-body as a teacher because I believed the children's needs were not being met and that the teachers were rarely respected or treated fairly, that I made myself ill. I did not feel ready to take on the system. I just wanted to teach.

I love teaching and I'm sure you do too. If you don't, then jump ship and find something that makes your heart sing. I believe there is nothing more magical than being in a classroom of young heart-minds and igniting their imagination or interest. Yes, the paper work is obscene, and the number-crunching often misses the point of education, but what would you rather be doing? And if you have an inspired way to reduce the red tape, offer your solutions and make it happen! I'm sure senior management would be very grateful for your solution-based thinking and positive contribution to the functioning of the whole school.

A government minister was heard to say *"Government should provide cash, support and silence". Will Ryan,* Leadership with a Moral Purpose

> *"Despite the fact that we all run at ninety miles an hour, education remains the slowest moving industry in England. Too much of the work carried out in our schools is based on a curriculum that does not meet the needs of children growing up in the modern world...The problem is that the curriculum is seen as the content of education rather than a source of discovery and fulfilment."*
>
> Will Ryan, *Leadership with a Moral Purpose.*

So I have learned over the years to stop arguing with reality. As Byron Katie says: *"When you argue with reality, you only lose one hundred percent of the time!"* Unless you are willing to take up the baton and run with your bug-bear to make a positive change, stop! You are only creating unnecessary stress for yourself. By all means explore ways in which you could do things differently or work with your department to address issues that frustrate or hinder teaching and learning, but avoid the incessant internal dialogue that repeatedly eats into you. It will make you sick! Instead, you may like to take time out to breathe, be still, and centre yourself. Take time to be grateful for everything that *is* working in your teaching and learning microcosm and release those stressful thoughts that do nothing to serve either your emotional health and well-being or that of your students. Ask the questions: "Where would I be without that stressful thought?"; "How would I feel without that stressful thought?"; "Whose business am I in?" If you want to learn more about breaking negative cycles of destructive thinking, look into *The Work* by Byron Katie. It's easy and simple to apply and it could possibly blow your mind! Failing that, simply follow *The Magician's Way...* focus on your Greatness, do what's obvious, teach and lead from Love.

If you do feel that you are working with a straitjacket on, my invitation is gently to unclip the buckles one at a time, and even if you cannot unclip them completely, you can at least loosen them a little. Begin exploring what you can do healthily to manipulate the mould. Get curious and ask what's already in place that will allow your creativity to flow and your teaching heart to sing. Give yourself permission to interpret the National Curriculum (or whatever strategy is being implemented in that moment!). Will Ryan reminds us that it is there only as a guideline, yet it has been taken on as gospel! Give yourself permission to take risks in your lessons. Your students will remember the unusual lessons, the exciting hands-on experiences, and the lessons that place the subject in the heart of their values so that they can make sense of it in their world in their terms.

Take a moment now to stop, breathe, and dive into your imagination. If there were no perceived restrictions in your subject area or in your teaching, what would you do? How would you teach? What would you do differently? If you were not afraid of criticism or reprimand for teaching outside the box, how and what would you do? Have fun and feel what it feels like to experience the new approach in your imagination. Why not have a department meeting and explore how you can get your creative juices flowing and return to what you know and love best?

And finally, remember to have fun! Learning is fun! Learning is more easily accessed and remembered when it is fun. Learning should be fun! There is an unspoken ethos that if your students are not working in silence or being quiet and still, that they are not learning. What if you could turn that unconscious belief inside-out and upside-down and embrace active, fun-filled learning?! The value of fun cannot be underestimated. When reassuring teachers who are afraid to have fun in the classroom during an Ofsted inspection, Will Ryan reminds them *"that they are not having fun, they are (deep breath) using positive emotions to access the limbic system to optimise dopamine secretion to facilitate autonomic learning"*. Relax and have fun as best you can in the circumstances you are in with the resources you have in each moment. Remember, you can't stop the waves but you can enjoy the ocean and all it offers as you surf.

"Clearly what is meant to be is.
The Peace is always in that."

Gangaji

Listen to Your Body

The most challenging experience in my early years of teaching was that I felt I had never done enough, or rather I felt there was always something more I could be doing. The reality was there *was* always something more that could be done. What I have gradually come to learn is that this is the nature of teaching. If you are keen to constantly challenge yourself, improve yourself as a teacher, and develop new ways to connect with your learners, there will always be something more you can do. There will always be another book you can read, another teaching article, another new method to experiment with and more legislation to get your head around. There will always be more ways to improve your classroom displays and demonstrate learning progress. But...

Here is my simple message. Learn to be okay with what is. If you are like me, and I am always striving to be the best I can be and give the best I can give to my students, develop the ability to loosen your reins and be okay with "good enough". You need to train yourself to stop and rest. You need to give yourself a break and accept sometimes that it will have to be good enough. I learnt this at the "failing" school I had the good fortune to teach in. I was put in a classroom that was not fit for purpose; there was dangerous machinery in the room and vices on the desk; the desks were cut, worn, and damaged, so it was very difficult to produce neat work, and any artwork attempted on them was likely to be sub-par; the room had not been used for quite a while, it was dirty and tatty. Not only did I need to address the environment, I also had to manage groups of boys who weren't used to high expectations, especially in my subject. Their behaviour needed serious guidance, as did their attitude. And this was just the tip of the iceberg. There were far more challenging issues within the department which I shall not divulge here.

All in all, I had my work cut out for me. I had a young family and I was dealing with some serious life-changing issues in my personal life as well. At this point in my career, I had to make the choice: do my best and set myself some boundaries, quit, or get sick. I wasn't prepared to revisit the latter, and I am not big on quitting. So this was one of the many gifts this particularly challenging school gave me. I learnt when to go home, and I set my boundaries around marking. I learnt to manage my time better and sometimes settle for less than my absolute best. I still turned my classroom into a haven of peace and inspirational learning and I still managed to create a stunning mural with my art club during lunch times. This is my invitation to do your best, be your best, and remember that sometimes you must pull back if you are to thrive, not just survive!

> *" Stop striving for perfection and*
> *settle for excellence."*
>
> Dr Topher Morrison

If you are feeling unwell, alter your lesson to accommodate your state. Give yourself permission to be flexible with your teaching and learning regime. Just as you instinctively know how to turn up or turn down the heat in your classroom for your children, depending on their energy levels, mood or concentration, so too can you readjust your input and output. As I became unwell in my first year at teaching and mentioned how exhausted I was feeling, my supportive head of faculty suggested I teach something that was more independent-learning focused. She gave me permission to ease up and let go. This came as a huge surprise for me. Over time, I understood the wisdom of this balance. This is why I am so keen to support and encourage all teachers, no matter where they are along their teaching path. She taught me that sometimes 50% of your best is still good enough. Sometimes just showing up, being present, and trusting what is, is enough. When appropriate and where necessary, give yourself the gentler option. You do not have to prove yourself all the time (even though it often feels like it!). Give yourself a break on all levels and avoid beating yourself up about it! Accept what is and what is required in that moment. Remember your outer circumstances are out of your control. You have no control over the weather, but you can create the weather in your classroom, even if you've walked in from a storm. Choose sunshine! And one of the best ways to do this is to give yourself permission to be human. If you need help, ask for it. If you need support, seek it out. Take action. Get advice. Don't wait until you are at breaking point. You are too important for that!

One NQT I trained recently wanted her feedback form to remain anonymous. She was afraid her head teacher would find out she felt overwhelmed. She didn't want to be perceived as unable to cope. The truth of the matter was that she was coping *and* she was struggling. There is such an unspoken curse around feeling stressed. What if you could begin to break this unhelpful cycle and create a support group or a forum for letting off steam or sharing concerns? It can be a place for reassurance and encouragement. If you do not feel able to reach out to your colleagues for whatever reason I highly recommend you seek help to manage the challenges you face. You may have a supportive team or welcoming staffroom; if so, great; if not, seek out someone you can confide in (professional or familial) and address the imbalance. There are services available. The Teacher Support Network (www.teachersupport.info) is a fantastic place to start. You could also check out the resources I am regularly making available online.

I am not suggesting there is a right way to deal with the obstacles you face. You know you best. You will know what feels right for you. If you are feeling overwhelmed right now, take a deep breath, go inside, and be still. Just listen. Wait, and the answers will be revealed. You will know what direction to go in. And if you are still unclear, phone a friend, ask the audience, or go for a 50/50 compromise. You'll be fine. Just hold on to your surfboard, ensure you're wearing your wetsuit, and have your shades and factor-50 at the ready!

CHAPTER NINE

Simple Steps

Simple Steps

"Give a man a fish and you can feed him for a day. Teach a man to fish and you feed him for a lifetime."

Chinese Proverb

Every Teacher Matters! No matter what your discipline, experience or title - from NQTs to ASTs (Advanced Skills Teacher) - you all play a crucial role in the development of education. Teachers come in all shapes and sizes. Some may be deemed "old school"; some may be perceived as avant-garde. Wherever you rest on the spectrum of teaching philosophy, know that you are amazing! You are extremely influential in the lives of young people, and your value is immeasurable. It is imperative that you take great care of yourself! The system as it stands does not take very good care of you. Unless you are lucky to work in a caring and supportive department, *YOU* are the only person that can look out for you. Even then, no-one can make you go to bed at a sensible time and no-one can make you eat healthy foods and take regular exercise to ensure your body is in good condition. No-one can make you address your stress if you don't want to!

You make a difference in the classroom. You make a difference in your school. You make a difference in your community, and you make a difference in your society. You! Each and every one of you who have been called to teach, called to inspire and ignite the minds and hearts of beautiful, impressionable and delicate souls. You are the one! Anthropologist Margaret Meade said: *"Never doubt that a small group of thoughtful committed citizens can change the world".* Without you, a vital component to our societal development and growth would be missing. It is your responsibility to take up the baton each term and bring your children alive with the possibilities of our world. You also have the responsibility to ensure you are fit for purpose! Emotionally fit not only to cope with the pressures of teaching life, but also emotionally resourced to manage the pain that you and the children may experience and find expressed (healthily or unhealthily) in the classroom. Ensure you are as physically fit as you can be. Teaching is a physically, mentally, and emotionally demanding job. It requires you to be healthy in mind and body. Put yourself first!

Take the oxygen first. Remember how, in the safety announcement on aeroplanes, the handsome flight attendant reminds you, in the event of an emergency, to place the oxygen mask on yourself first before helping anyone else? If you tend to the needs of others first and you run out of air to breathe, you will not be much use to them when you are unconscious! You will not be there for them in the ensuing crisis. So do what's obvious and take the oxygen first so you are in a fit state, the right state for teaching. Ensure you get enough rest and enough fresh air. Take yourself into nature regularly, ensure you bring yourself out of your mind and get into your body. Jump, dance, and strut your funky stuff in whatever way works for you. And if you feel too exhausted to do it, focus on how great you will feel after the exercise! Alternatively, have a refreshing, gentle swim. You know what I'm talking about!!! Make it fun and move your body in a way that makes you smile! Ensure your mind is stretched in the way it loves, and ensure your mind is given space and time to stop! Give yourself time to be still, relax, and breathe deeply. Bring your attention to your inner life and fill up your internal love tank! When you do this, the parts of you that are frantically being pulled in all directions will soften and relax. There is a deeper knowing when a

Mindful connection is made. There is a "surrender" that takes place that will provide you with insight and wisdom that is impossible to put into words.

Being aware of your mind-body-heart connection and ensuring you support all parts of who you are will ensure you can sustain a long, happy, and healthy teaching career. Bringing your awareness to the present moment and placing your focus on it will create opportunities to do things differently. At first it will bring simplicity into your teaching practice, then it will bring new ideas and right-brain thinking, which will nurture your creative problem-solving inside and outside the classroom. With practise, you will find there is a natural rhythm to your teaching experience which will help you go with the flow and manage the highs and lows of each moment. Criticism and unhelpful judgments are lessened and the inner critic quietens. You can hear the words and address the judgements in a healthy way. You have the power to dismiss or embrace the thoughts. You can choose. You can choose to take healthy action and experience the internal (and external) feedback as just another opportunity to learn and grow, not only as a teacher but as a human being. Remember you are always doing the very best you can with the resources you have at that time and so are your students. It may not seem like it sometimes, but this is what I believe.

To enjoy a long, happy and abundant teaching career, you will have the opportunity every day to perform the extraordinary juggling act that you have chosen to embrace. You will focus on creating sunshine in your classroom, no matter what stormy seas you may have sailed in on. You will connect with your Power Breath and all other internal resources and techniques to support your mind and body. You will employ your natural gifts to centre yourself before, during, and after class. You will be Mindful of your influence and how you can affect (positively or negatively) each and every child in your care. You will be so finely in tune with the present moment that you will be more able to meet your needs and the needs of each child. You will love your job so much, even with all the bureaucracy and heinous measuring, that you will keep the challenges in perspective and remain balanced in your outlook and attitude. Your focus is always on the best end-result for your learning family, and that includes you and your colleagues. When you are fully in balance and inspired by your personal teaching vision, your vocation will become your vacation!

Effective teaching will occur naturally as you focus on having fun throughout the learning experience. You will be so aware of how making learning fun will draw your busy little bees to your honey pot! There will be a lot less resistance to the learning challenges if the student feels relaxed. If he believes he will have fun in your classroom, even if the work is challenging, he is more likely to stay present. You employ lots of fun and simple techniques throughout the learning session to invite and keep your learners on task and in the present moment. After the initial "this is weird", or more likely "you're weird, Miss", your students will embrace or at least accept that this is the way they do it in your class. Hopefully, your entire school will embrace Mindful Self Management and so you will feel less of an alien. Even if you are considered a little alien, remember children are curious about things that are a little different. Even if they are vocally critical or sceptical, be present to this and stay focused on your end-result: happy, relaxed, and healthy learners.

Your L plates will remain securely fastened throughout your teaching life, bringing fresh new ideas and insights into your teaching practice as you continue to learn from other practitioners and inspiring authorities. You teach by example, leading learning by demonstrating how and what *you* are learning too. Each day offers you fresh opportunities to learn new ideas and new ways of thinking. Each student will provide opportunities to test your skills and will help you fine-tune your behaviour management, approaches to teaching and learning, and ways you communicate. You will experiment with your most valuable tool after your breath, your body! You will be aware of how you hold your body to communicate your message. You will ensure your spine is aligned and that your eye contact is regular and appropriate. You will be acutely aware of how your body language and facial expressions influence and affect your students and their attitude to learning. Your demeanour creates the weather.

You will bring yourself into balance before class and have the internal resources to re-balance yourself after a situation in the classroom. You will continue to bring your awareness of each challenge and explore what you could do differently or how confrontation could be avoided or managed in the future. With your Mindful approach, you will be able to assess the situation without judgement and simply address what could be learned from the experience for both you and the child, children, or staff involved. Each challenge will provide an opening for you to grow, learn, and become a more Mindful, efficient, and effective teacher.

Your L plates will serve to remind you that there can be no room for complacency in the classroom, as every new lesson brings new choices and challenges for both you and your students. Every moment is a new possibility. Every moment is a fresh opportunity to plant seeds in the minds of your learners so flowers can grow. As a Mindful Teacher, you have the chance to notice any weeds sprouting in the garden of your mind and the minds of your students, and you will develop the understanding necessary to get weeding and pull out the unhelpful thoughts by the roots so that they do not return. You know that if you clear your garden bed and leave it, weeds will soon grow back, no matter how deeply you dug! Instead, you can replace them with flowers and you can be the best example of how to tend the garden of your mind for your children.

Managing behaviour and the emotions that naturally occur with them will be a gift for your personal development. It will give you the opportunity to expand the Mindful qualities you want to develop in yourself and will improve your Mindful approach to your students, your teaching, and your life. It will develop your patience, compassion, and humility when dealing with challenging behaviour. You are more likely to be open-minded and willing to perceive the behaviour as a symptom of negative internal dialogue than a wilful disobedience of the rules! When heartfully approaching unpleasant and undesirable behaviour, your natural inclination will be to acknowledge and possibly address the core issue and "pain" beneath the behaviour, rather than simply halting the behaviour. In the real world, I understand this can be very difficult to implement, especially if there is a subculture of aggressive and unruly behaviour within the school. However, one small step each day towards an empathetic approach to your students and the myriad of frustrations they encounter on a day-to-day basis will make a significant impact.

Everything about Mindful teaching stems from a heart-centred approach. Compassion and a heartful attitude to your students is a healthier and kinder approach to successful learning, clear communication, and healthy relationships. If you think this is too soft and fluffy, simply explore the statistics concerning suicide rates in young people, especially young men. Children and young people need all the love, support and guidance they can get, even and especially when they think they don't need or want it. The U.K. riots in August 2011 highlighted the discontent in so many young people. It is a very challenging time; you will influence and impact their choices and experiences for the rest of their lives. Next time you're in a staff meeting, having a social with friends or at any group function, ask which teacher inspired your career choice or attitude to learning and which teacher turned you off and why. There will be a correlation between your attitude and theirs. Were they dismissive or judgemental, maybe unwilling to listen to your perspective? Maybe they were unapproachable or unfair. They may simply have been dull, loquacious, or unhappy. Remember the key is to provide a happy, relaxed, and kind learning environment. It is a fine line to balance heartful classroom management with boundary setting and discipline, but it can be done with practice and thoughtfulness. It simply takes time and care to implement, just like learning to ride a bicycle. You have to get your balance first and then push off when you're ready. You need to gain momentum, and you need to trust that you can take both feet off the ground and keep pedalling! When you fall off, you dust yourself off and climb back on. You may feel a little shaky, but it will be worth it in the end. The freedom, fun and joy that mastering cycling brings is immense! Being able to get from A to B safely, swiftly, and independently brings a whole new realm of possibilities. Cycling through unchartered lands brings exhilaration and happiness!

The freedom, fun and joy that mastering Mindful teaching brings are riches beyond compare! Exploring unchartered landscapes of the mind, both yours and your students, will open new doors and new paradigms in teaching and learning. You and your students will feel free to open your hearts to new ways of self-expression, communication, and personal development.

You will understand how important leading by example really is: that rushing, pushing through, striving, and efforting may not be the best ways to produce meaningful results or measure success. I'm not suggesting hard work and effort isn't involved in performing tasks; what I am suggesting is that if the framework and mindset towards the task is balanced, the task will seem and feel easier. The willingness to pursue the task set and to persevere when it gets tough is more likely to arise in your students if they have a Mindful understanding. This understanding will undoubtedly affect your attitude towards the way you teach, the methods you employ to get their attention, and the manner in which you maintain their attention and focus.

During INSET workshops, I offer techniques to implement throughout your lesson to keep you calm and centred, to keep your students on task and inspired, and to maintain their concentration and progress. There are many ways you can gently introduce Mindful learning into your classroom, no matter what age you are teaching. Each technique will not only serve your students' behaviour, attitudes to learning, concentration and listening skills, it will also undoubtedly serve your behaviour, attitudes to teaching and learning, concentration and listening skills! Every time you implement a supportive Mindful Awareness Practice (MAP) into your lesson, you are creating an opportunity to make space for yourself. This expansive approach to teaching and learning will serve to generate an ambience of wholesome respect and enjoyment. The "head space" you create for your children will provide "head space" for you. This is imperative for your health and well-being in a hectic education system of full timetables, loaded schemes of work, and content-heavy lesson plans. The time you make for yourself to breathe, take a moment, and become fully present with your class, will enable you to teach more effectively, support yourself in stressful situations (and we all have those challenging moments, classes, or students that test us!), and manage the ongoing pressures of 21st-century schooling.

Mindful methods provide an alternative approach to teaching and learning. They inspire trust, generate a deeper connection, and develop creativity and imagination. They enhance parts of the brain that will stimulate creative problem-solving, deep relaxation, hopefulness, and peace. The mind-body-heart connection is used to greatest advantage: rather than working against natural resources, it taps into your natural body wisdom. Your imagination and ability to bring your awareness to the present moment, to your breath, or to wherever you want to draw your attention, is a life-long tool for mental and emotional health.

Your ability to implement MAP (Mindful Awareness Practises) into your lessons in a completely different way and direct your focus will help you manage your stress as well as the challenges your students may face in entering the learning experience. No matter what the age or ability, if your students are inhibited, nervous or anxious about what they are learning in that moment, they will feel tension rising in their body and will find it harder to concentrate or integrate the learning. As a Mindful teacher, you will have the tools not only to read the signs of your students, you will also have the techniques up your sleeve to communicate healthily, help change their state, and support them as they ride the waves. Together, you will be able to surf in a safe and supportive environment and know that if either you or a child falls off their board, there will be mechanisms and strategies to help you climb back on and enjoy the ocean once again.

There are two parts to taking good care of yourself. The first part is the practical day-to-day self-care of your body, and the second part is the inner landscape of your mind. Return to the basics in Chapter 3 reminding you how to take the oxygen first.

Throughout the book, I have covered some key techniques and concepts to support you and your teachings:

- The Serenity Jar
- The Diamond Within
- Taking Down the Armour
- Power Breath
- Breathe and Smile

Revisit and practise regularly for optimum health.

To close, I would simply like to thank you for reading this book. I never cease to marvel at teachers who take time out to read research and endeavour continually to improve themselves and their teaching skills. Thank you for being open to exploring a new way. Thank you for being willing to expand your horizons and to explore outside the box. Thank you for considering new possibilities and new arenas for the mind. Thank you for opening your heart to the children you have taught and the many fortunate children you will teach in the future. If you take nothing from this book other than recognising how valuable you are in the world, then I have done my job. If you also take away how important, influential, and responsible you are, then all the better. If by some miracle, I have convinced you to sample the wonders of Mindfulness, to explore the possibilities of *being* rather than *doing,* and to bring the world of Stillness into your classroom, then I will indeed die a happy teacher! It has been my utmost pleasure sharing my thoughts with you. The more I write, the more I want to share. There is so much more I have yet to inspire you with. Present-Moment teaching and learning is the new paradigm to guide teachers and students on their unique path of self-understanding, personal development, and delightful discovery.

I now invite you to stop with me just one last time and consider what you really want from your teaching life and what your end-result is, not simply for your students but also for yourself. In an era of target-setting, chronic testing, learning outcomes, exam results, and league tables, what specifically do *you* want to achieve? Just take three deep, welcoming breaths and allow your vision to evolve. The answer you have for yourself will be fingerprint-unique to you. The answer you have for your children and young people will be heart-centred. What if you not only inspired the minds of your students but also awakened your entire school community to approach teaching Mindfully? What if you guided your students to be well-rounded, kind, compassionate, and creative? What if you invited them to be non-judgemental, Mindful, heart-ful human beings that could not only cope with the challenges of life, but were also inspired to follow their hearts, to dare to dream, and to focus on their diamond within, just like you? You have the power to make this possible!

"Teachers open the door. You enter by yourself."

Chinese Proverb

For all doubting Toms, I shall share a magic moment with you from my prison class this year. A new learner said he wasn't going to stay in the class if it was all that "weird lying-down breathing crap". One of my course graduates replied: "Listen mate, THIS SHIT REALLY WORKS!" Need I say more! Another man testified that it was "almost better than sex!" What can I say; you'll have to try it for yourself!

About the Author

Kathryn Lovewell specialises in emotional resilience, having taught inside and outside mainstream education for the last 20 years. She trains Senior Leaders, Teachers, NQTs (and students) to manage their stress healthily and to effectively cope with the ever increasing emotional and psychological demands of teaching. Kathryn's mission is to reduce stress in schools and promote well being. She is committed to heart-centred teaching and learning, where education embraces the wellbeing of every teacher and student.

For more information please visit **www.kathrynlovewell.com**

Emotional Resilience Training For Teachers

Testimonials

"Kathryn's book has such a powerful role to play. If every child matters, then it must follow as night follows day that every teacher matters."

Professor Felicia A Huppert,
Professor of Psychology, Director of the Well-being Institute, University of Cambridge.

"Every Teacher Matters is the future of education! In her book Kathryn not only offers practical ways of engaging and generating a sustainable, progressive and positive learning environment, but clearly demonstrates why teachers deserve to be actively acknowledged and supported in the vital role they play in building a healthy society and economy. This book promotes an idea whose time has come. I hope it will serve as a very long overdue call to arms to governments, senior leaders and governors everywhere."

Julian Stanley,
Group Chief Executive, Teacher Support Network.

"This creative, inspirational book provided me with the motivation, comfort and revitalisation that I needed to help me through my NQT year. A must read for teachers everywhere! Thank you!"

Julia Panchkowry,
NQT.

"It's a pity this book was not available when I was doing my teacher training 16 years ago! I could have done with someone like Kathryn to guide and inspire me back then. She is a diamond in the world of education! Thank goodness teachers are finally getting the support and recognition they deserve."

Yvonne Williams,
Adult Learning Lecturer.

"It would be hard to imagine a more inspiring book than this one. If every teacher had the chance to read it, they and every child they teach would benefit immeasurably".

Kate Hopkinson ,
Director of Inner Skills; Senior Research Associate, London School of Economics.
Designated expert in cognitive science for the European Commission.

Testimonials

"Some of the greatest influencers in life are our teachers. They have the power to shape our characters, point us purposefully in positive directions, and inspire us to liberate our own innate shining potential. I am so grateful that finally a book has been written to empower these "Gardeners of Souls" with practical liberating tools to free up their lives, to discover their own value and to live life to the fullest. Finally someone is giving back to these most essential people in our lives: Our Teachers."

Brandon Bays,
International Best Selling Author of The Journey® and The Journey for Kids.

"This is such an inspirational book which is a must-read for all teachers to give you practical tools to look after your emotional, physical and mental health."

Dr Marilyn Glenville PhD,
the UK's leading nutritionist specialising in women's health and author of 'Fat around the Middle'.

"Every Teacher Matters is a must read for anyone interested in understanding more about how mindfulness practice can benefit both teachers and students. Kathryn Lovewell brings the concept of the Mindful Teacher to life through a mixture of thoughtful prose and well thought out and accessible mindfulness exercises. Her passion for teaching and mindfulness make this an enjoyable and engaging read, and I hope Every Teacher Matters will inspire others to incorporate mindfulness into their workplace."

Dr Shanida Nataraja,
Scientific Director/Author of The Blissful Brain.

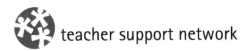 teacher support network

The **Teacher Support Network** passionately believes in teachers. It is the only charity providing teachers with emotional and practical advice throughout their careers. They help all teachers at any type of school at any stage of their career; from trainees to retired teachers. They also help the families and dependents of teachers.

Their work complements that of the unions and addresses both crisis intervention and prevention. From counseling to money management, they offer support during times of crisis. Through policy and research they aim to improve teacher status and recognition.

www.teachersupport.info

For every book sold, a percentage of the proceeds will go to the Teacher Support Network.